"From the Inside"

The question is "How many?" How many family breakdowns, wayward children, diseases, addictions, depressions, backslidings, financial failures, separations, rages, violent outbursts, and countless other problems brought to pastors, doctors, clinicians, psychiatrists and government agencies are actually rooted in spiritual issues that have not been dealt with? How many occurrences in life are actually issues of salvation and deliverance? How many are a lack of dominion over spiritual and demonic power? How many of a person's myriads of troubles in this life are really about areas in life where they lack spiritual authority? Things such as these are not always about physical strength or difficult circumstances, but about spiritual weakness and giving-up the battle.

The late M. Scott Peck was an American Psychiatrist and author of the popular book, *The Road Less Traveled* (1978). He was practicing psychiatry when the movie, *The Exocist*, was released. He became interested in exorcism and published *People of the Lie* in 1983. He says that many of people's problems are explainable in common psychiatric practice. He adds, however, that he has "seen the face of evil."

Have you ever fought un-conquerable powers that have in some manner deformed your life? Are there things unseen that torment and drive you to strange behavior? Has your life been turned upside-down and your hopes dashed so you cannot see a way out?

When you decide to set your will to be a Christian and live as a Christian in obedience then you establish a culture of dominion.

Faith must be the story-line of the life you live. Faith must be the boundary or border that encases all that is allowed in our life. Faith, however, is not religion.

Today's Christian is often building a life of materialism that does not provide a frame for understanding this life or the life to come.

An essential part of who you are is the story of where you came from.

It was a culture that had a long reach. It cost them dominion and their promised inheritance. It didn't have to cost them.

Job confesses he has learned what he did not know. What he had learned in conventional instruction and theology (doctrine) he now knows personally, intimately and in reality.

Dominion is a spiritual dimension and quality of life that is primarily inside. It is essential though often invisible.

People commonly see money, wealth and power as their security. They think these are able to deliver them from any difficulty in life. Money dictates many decisions in life.

The flesh you spare today is the flesh that will destroy you tomorrow. The deception of thinking time is on your side is common. It is not true.

Sometimes it is hard to grasp the importance of prayer. Daniel's prayer transforms his understanding of God. It becomes more than doctrine and theology. It becomes more than a calculus or balance sheet of right and wrong. In crisis we often learn more about God. God is much more than we assumed.

How to Gain Control of Your Life

Deliverance
to

Dominion

Joe C. Campbell

John W. Gooding

DELIVERANCE TO DOMINION
How to Gain Control of Your Life

Copyright © 2019 by Joseph C. Campbell and John W. Gooding

All rights reserved. No part of this book may be used or reproduced in any manner without written permission except in the case of brief exerpts in critical reviews or articles.

Scripture taken from the New King James Version®.
Copyright©1982 by Thomas Nelson, Inc. Used by permission. All rights reserved.

Information address:

Joe C. Campbell, P.O. Box 305, Chandler, AZ 85244
John W. Gooding, P.O. Box 268, Globe, AZ 85502

Library of Congress Cataloging-in-Publication Data has been applied for.

ISBN-13: 978-1-7332271-0-0

DEDICATION:

For all the pastors, pioneers and disciples
of the Christian Fellowship worldwide.

TABLE OF CONTENTS

CHAPTER 1
LEVIATHAN—THAT TWISTING SERPENT 1

CHAPTER 2
THE NECESSARY DISTINCTION 23

CHAPTER 3
DO YOU HAVE DOMINION? 49

CHAPTER 4
"THE 35": DECISIONS MAKE FOR DESTINY ..71

CHAPTER 5
YOU ARE WHAT YOU SPEAK 87

CHAPTER 6
SO QUICKLY TURNED 113

CHAPTER 7
THE ALGORITHM OF DOMINION 135

CHAPTER 8
BORN FOR DOMINION 151

CHAPTER 9
EPILOGUE 167

REFERENCES
CHAPTER NOTES 175

PREFACE

This is a book about dominion. It is about how to walk, live and lead your family into dominion.

One of the great tragedies in the Bible occurs after God went to great lengths to deliver his people out of Egypt. He performed signs, wonders and miracles to bring about their deliverance. He established them under the blood of Christ when death coursed through Egypt. God parted the waters of the Red Sea and destroyed their enemies who tried to hunt them down. Yet, tragically, they died in the wilderness. They never possessed their inheritance. They never lived in destiny. Exodus' great lessons are life can deal you bitter blows, engulf you with enemies, swallow up your resources twist your desires, and drown you in sorrows. How? A lack of dominion.

How many are in the church today without an ability to process the events of life in dominion. They are saved and have been powerfully delivered and yet never seem to arrive or live in their kingdom inheritance. Is it true of you? Do you spend your life wandering in the wilderness?

Is there an answer? Yes! In every event of life you can have the upper hand by walking in dominion. This is good news. Jesus did not deliver you to die in the wilderness. There is a way to walk, live and lead in dominion. May this book inspire and instruct you to move from deliverance to dominion.

Joseph C. Campbell
June 2019

PREFACE

I think most who play chess understand it is played in the mind. It is a mind game. But it is not "mind over matter." The Devil has proven to be a Master in mind games. He played well in defeating God's people in the wilderness. He has proven to be formidable in Israel's national life.

Without question the Exodus was one of the most important and stunning deliverances in world history. Equally stunning, following the Exodus over six million men, age twenty and above fit for war perished in the wilderness. The reason is the theme of this book, they lacked dominion.

It was not the only exodus for the Hebrews. Nehemiah and Ezra led the nation out of the Babylonian captivity. When the "holy Seed" reached Jerusalem and Ezra read the law of God they both wept and rejoiced for all God had done.

This is often the picture of deliverance. Great joy and weeping for joy are common with deliverance. It is the story of revival as well. In the wilderness the children of God built a fabulous tabernacle. Israel, upon returning from the Baylonian captivity, had rebuilt the walls and the temple. Ezra fell on his face before God in shame and humiliation. The holy seed had become mixed with the morals and habits of the pagan world around them. In revivals there are often magnificent churches and social structures established. The bright moment—for it seems but a moment—of deliverance is dashed in the absence of dominion over the wickedness of the world.

It is often commented that revivals last, at best, a generation. The figure is usually about forty years and then the revival wanes. It is worn down because the affairs of life are not processed properly, and the demonic powers wear out the saints of God. What is the answer? What was the answer for the Jesus People Movement of the seventies and eighties? Millions of young people were powerfully delivered from drugs and alcohol but soon found themselves caught up in the immorality and perversions of the progressive new social structure.

Dominion is purchased by a life submitted to God. The demonic world is relentless in seeking to overthrow the believer by taking advantage of common circumstances and twisting them into false conclusions about life, about God, about the church and about the future. Many souls do not process tragic or catastrophic events with a pathway to the future. They succumb to making these events the defining—and finishing—moment of their lives. The rest of their life is seen through the lens of one or two setbacks, tragedies or failures.

The Devil is not a match for God. Here, in these pages are stories of those who did not succumb to the strategies of hell. They found ways to move ahead to powerful and important destinies. The hellish assaults in times of difficulty, confusion and perplexity were cast down and demolished by remaining steadfast in faith and faithfulness. These stories can be your story.

The book you are reading can be seen in three basic sections. Chapters 1-3 establish the definition and meaning of dominion. In particular, they reference the Exodus from Egypt. Chapters 4-6 give examples of the crucial issues in the face of demonic assault. Chapter four gives us the crucial story of Ruth and her mother-in-law Naomi. Her decision was made in the uncertainty that follows tragedy. In chapter five we follow the understanding of James and the importance of the story we tell. Chapter six is about the allocation of resources. It is about how you can have dominion in finances. Chapters 7-9 are aimed at practical things persons can do to make dominion an active part of the Christian life. They are the spiritual dynamics that bring God into the arena of your personal life. Whenever and wherever you surrender to God in your life dominion can be established. You can win over the powers of darkness that torment, drive and divert your mind. You can live in God's peace.

A cursory look at current and recent books reveals a dearth of books related to dominion. There are, and have been especially during the Jesus

People Movement, good and valuable books on spiritual warfare. Certainly, dominion involves that element. We remain convinced, however, that a look at dominion will be a significant contribution to all who seek to make the pilgrimage across the wilderness to a destiny in the Promised Land.

John W. Gooding
June 2019

ACKNOWLEDGEMENTS

No book is the work of one person—or even two. Many thanks and appreciation go to the numerous pastors who read parts of the manuscript and various chapters for comment. Special thanks to Pastor Wayman Mitchell for encouragement to pursue the project. Special thanks to Larry Beauregard for setting up the pages and format of the book, to James Rosario for the cover design and to the staff of The Door Church of Chandler, Arizona. We are deeply indebted to the congregations of The Door Church, and the Globe Christian Center in Globe, Arizona for their release of time and resources for this publication. It is, of course, our responsibility for errors of omission and commission in the book.

CHAPTER 1

LEVIATHAN—THAT TWISTING SERPENT

We wrestle ... against spiritual hosts of wickedness.

"I wonder, in eternity, if we'll see how many things were spiritual?" The question came up in a conversation between pastors Joe Campbell and Wayman Mitchell. How many times was more happening than could be seen in the circumstances. How many times were the real issues clouded and confused? How many times was there misleading body language, poor communication, words that twisted and misdirected, and words that did not represent the real issue.

We wonder how many of the issues people bring to a pastor, doctor, clinician or counselor are spiritual? They are not just about their circumstances or physical health? There are issues that cannot be fixed by changing their circumstances or taking pills. How many are spiritual? Unless they are dealt with, the crisis or trouble cannot be helped. Paul said we do not wrestle with flesh and blood. Yet, it seems people are often doing just that. People fight one another rather than engage in the spiritual issues of their soul. Jesus cast out unclean spirits. Daniel's prayers were resisted by a demonic power. John writes about a spirit of Jezebel, the antichrist, divination, infirmity and bondage. The ministry of the New Testament is filled with deliverance and healing. There is a spiritual war. Many talk about it, few engage in it. Fewer engage in it with any confidence.

The question is "How many?" How many family breakdowns, wayward children, diseases, addictions, depressions, backslidings, financial failures, separations, rages, violent outbursts, and countless other problems brought to pastors, doctors, clinicians, psychiatrists and government agencies are actually rooted in spiritual issues that have not been dealt with? How many occurrences in life are actually issues of salvation and deliverance? How many are a lack of dominion over spiritual and demonic power? How many of a person's myriads of troubles in this life are really about areas in life where they lack spiritual authority? Things such as these are not always about physical strength or difficult circumstances, but rather are about spiritual weakness.

Many pastors and counselors understand there is an unseen world. What you see is not all there is. The world is not just one of myth, imagination and fantasy. It is a real and powerful world. Many people give token acknowledgement to a god or force somewhere. For most people, life is about the here and now. Those who deal with people who have problems often recognize there is another layer of "spiritual activity" that has affected their world.

The late M. Scott Peck was an American Psychiatrist and author of the popular book, *The Road Less Traveled* (1978). He was practicing psychiatry when the movie, *The Exorcist*, was released. He became interested in exorcism and published *People of the Lie* in 1983. He says that many of people's problems are explainable in common psychiatric practice. He adds, however, that he has "seen the face of evil."[1]

When Scott Peck saw "the face of evil" he was in deliverance services for two different people. He says,

> As a hard headed scientist—which I assume myself to be—I can explain 95 percent of what went on in these two cases by traditional psychiatric dynamics.... But I am left with a critical 5 percent I cannot explain in such ways. I am left with the supernatural—or better yet, the subnatural.

He continued to describe the event.

> When the demonic finally spoke ... an expression appeared. It was an incredibly contemptuous grin of utter hostile malevolence. I have spent many hours before a mirror trying to imitate it without the slightest success.... The patient [his term] suddenly resembled a

writhing snake of great strength, viciously attempting to bite the team members. More frightening than the writhing [twisting] body, however, was the face.

Peck continued to describe the impact this had on him.

[W]hat upset me the most was the extraordinary sense of a fifty-million-year-old heaviness I received from this serpentine being. Almost all ... were convinced they were in the presence of something absolutely alien and inhuman.[2]

In both of Peck's observations the deliverance ended with the departure of this *presence* from the room.

We wrestle against spiritual power. In Isaiah 27:1, Leviathan is a "gliding" or "coiling (twisting) serpent." Isaiah uses a reptile or serpent of the sea to describe a spiritual power. Literally, Leviathan is a spiritual beast. This kind of illustration is common in biblical usage. Maarten J. Paul says in *Dictionary of Old Testament Theology and Exegesis*:

The Israelites used well-known emotive language and put a new meaning into it. They used the language of Babylonian myth to new purposes. For example, Isaiah, in need of strong imagery to cap his vision of God's victory over sin, oppression, and death, seizes on the Leviathan story and makes it say something much more profound than it had ever said before.[3]

The most explicit descriptions of Leviathan are found in Job 40-41. Usually, commentators take it as referring to a crocodile or a whale. Leviathan is a creature of the deep. This creatures represents demonic forces. In the ancient world the demonic often appears portrayed in animal form. Leviathan is a demonic entity.

Isaiah calls Leviathan the twisting serpent (ESV, NRSV). Leviathan is difficult to defeat. It is gliding (NIV), thrashing as it flees (MSG) and a swiftly moving (NLT) spirit escaping the sword.

Leviathan is an opportunist. It's a spirit that is quick to get involved and exploit any weakness, setback or circumstance that is difficult to handle. It manifests in a crisis. This demonic power causes one to misread events.

Leviathan is impervious to human weapons. In Job 41, God challenges Job to prove his mastery over this great creature. It is symbolic of cosmic forces hostile to God's rule. Since Job cannot subdue Leviathan, he is in no position to challenge God. In Job 41:4, God mockingly asks Job, "Will [Leviathan] make a covenant with you? Will you take [Leviathan] as a servant forever?" God is asking Job if he really thinks he can tame Leviathan. Does Job really believe he can make Leviathan a servant or bend his will?

The set of Old Testament words that describe iniquity are drawn from the same words used for twisting (Renn, 591; Richards, 566). Iniquity is a twisting dynamic. Something happens when one's mind or spirit gets twisted. It is not just your neighbor or circumstances. It is your mind. It is a demonic twisting of the mind. It is seen in 1 Samuel 20:30. Saul, in a fit of pique, describes Jonathan's mother as a perverse and rebellious woman. She is twisted. Again, in Proverbs 12:8, "twisted" describes a man with a warped mind. In other places it is used to describe persons who lack insight. It describes a perverted spirit or perverted heart. Leviathan's twisting affects the mind, vision, and the actions of believers.

The twisting serpent rages against the stable and godly mind. It manifests in uncharacteristic behavior. It overpowers a façade of "having it all together." One pastor in 1990, was involved in a church rebellion. In a meeting he literally lost his "I have it all together." Some described it as going "ballistic." This was not the event of a moment although it may have looked that way. No, somewhere he had opened a door or given a place in his mind to this twisting spirit. The issues were twisted in his heart. His motives twisted his view of life and leadership.

"My name is Ishmael." This is one of the most famous opening lines of a novel. It is in Herman Melville's 1851 novel, *Moby Dick*. Ishmael is the novel's narrator. He documents the whaling ship's Captain, Ahab, and his struggle with the great white whale, *Moby Dick*. Ahab, in a prior encounter with *Moby Dick*, lost his leg (bit off at the knee by the great beast) and had it replaced by a piece of carved whalebone. He refers to it as his "peg." The interplay of the physical and spiritual is often graphically illustrated in classic novels and movies.

Ahab, in the novel, struggles with powers that he does not see or understand. He'll go to his watery grave because he cannot deal with his traumatic past. It hurt him physically and emotionally. He is fighting in his flesh against a great beast he is unable to control. He will perish. Melville's novel is a story of a man held captive or enslaved to a demonic power and obsession. Melville illustrates, in *Moby Dick*, a spiritual power that enslaved the entire life of his character, Ahab. One of the reasons *Moby Dick* is a classic is because it describes a common struggle in life.

Certainly, we do not wrestle with a great whale. We do, however, wrestle with spiritual powers of darkness and the present evil age. We wrestle with the twisting spirit of another spiritual beast, Leviathan. The struggle often manifests in spoken words. Ishmael narrates Ahab's words.

> "Aye, aye! It was that accursed white whale that razeed [*sic*] me; made a poor pegging lubber of me for ever and a day!" Then tossing both arms, with measureless imprecations he shouted out: "Aye, aye! and I'll chase him round Good Hope, and round the Horn, and round the Norway Maelstrom, and round perdition's flames before I give him up. And this is what ye have shipped for, men! to chase that white whale on both sides of land, and over all sides of earth, till he spouts black blood and rolls fin out."

Ahab is driven. Ahab is filled with the venom of hatred, blame, revenge and rage. "He has made me a poor pegging lubber," or he has "crippled" me "forever." Ahab is willing to chase this great whale that deformed him around the Cape of Good Hope, and the around the Horn. He'll go through the violent waters of Norway, and the fires of hell if necessary, to find and fight Moby Dick. Ahab is driven to a final chase and his ultimate demise.

"Towards thee I roll, thou all-destroying but unconquering [sic] whale; to the last I grapple with thee; from hell's heart I stab at thee; for hate's sake I spit my last breath at thee."

Many people experience powers beyond themselves. Powers that create trouble, anxiety, torments and circumstances that test their very will to live. Like Ahab, despite defeat and setback, they still believe that they have the strength in themselves to come out victorious. This is a popular cultural narrative. "You can be whatever you want to be," and, "You can write your own story." The world says you can "dream your way to success."

Have you ever fought un-conquerable powers that have in some manner deformed your life? Are there things unseen that torment and drive you to strange behavior? Has your life been turned upside-down and your hopes dashed so you cannot see a way out? Ahab is on his last voyage. Are you on your last voyage? He still believes he can conquer the powers that rage in and against his life. He believes that he, within his flesh, has the power to defeat the great beast of the deep. He believes he alone can defeat the forces crashing like a tsunami against his life. Do you believe you can gain the upper hand in your flesh and wisdom?

Many—perhaps you—have found the answers to life's issues elusive. Like Ahab, you have found your personal efforts thwarted. Perhaps you are defeated. You are beaten in the game of life by things you don't understand and have no answers for. Often people cry out, even cry out to God, "Why me?" We wonder what is wrong with us and ask why things always fall apart? Even the successful and those who seem to enjoy the things of life are lonely, seek psychiatric help, and often fall to self-destructive addictions or perversions. Like Ahab, people are driven to fight against their demons.

Usually it is a fight with little success. John Meachem's recent book is *The Soul of America: The Battle for Our Better Angels*. The phrase is taken from Abraham Lincoln's first Inaugural address. It refers to the terrible sword that cut through the nation during the Civil War. A lost job, the collapse of a marriage, financial loss, children that fall into trouble with addictions or criminal behavior can slash across a stable life like a sword and plunge the mind and heart into turmoil. A natural disaster can wipe out years of savings, planning and efforts. What do you do? How do you think? What transpires in your mind when life appears to be set against you?

There is another universe besides the flesh and blood world. We live and interact with it every day. There is a spiritual universe that parallels this physical world. It is spiritual, but it also interacts with the physical world and the physical body. Paul writes about it in 2nd Corinthians 10.

> For though we walk in the flesh, we do not war according to the flesh. 4 For the weapons of our warfare are not carnal but mighty in God for pulling down strongholds, 5 casting down arguments and every high thing that exalts itself against the knowledge of God, bringing every thought into captivity to the obedience of Christ, 6 and being ready to punish all disobedience when your obedience is fulfilled. (2 Corinthians 10:3-5)

Ephesians also deals with this parallel world of the spirit.

> Finally, my brethren, be strong in the Lord and in the power of His might. 11 Put on the whole armor of God, that you may be able to stand against the wiles of the devil. 12 For we do not wrestle against flesh and blood, but against principalities, against powers, against the rulers of the darkness of this age, against spiritual hosts of wickedness in the heavenly places ... taking the shield of faith with which you will be able to quench all the fiery darts of the wicked one. (Ephesians 5:10-12, 16)

Much of 1st John is about the surging power of the demonic rising in and against the church in the last days. The lust of the flesh, the lust of the eyes, and the pride of life are the hallmarks of Leviathan. Listen to John, who writes in chapter 2:

> Little children, it is the last hour; and as you have heard that the Antichrist is coming, even now many antichrists have come, by which we know that it is the last hour. 19 They went out from us, but they were not of us; for if they had been of us, they would have

continued with us; but they went out that they might be made manifest, that none of them were of us. (1 John 2:18-19)

Who are "they" who went out? They were believers whose minds had become captivated by the twisting strength of arguments and imaginations against God and his people. Biblically, Leviathan describes the anti-authority nature of the demonic world. Leviathan is self-willed. The demonic exerts its powers against the mind of the believer. It cannot be overcome simply in positive confession or "I think I can." It is a spirit of lawlessness.

The biblical Naomi was Ruth's mother-in-law. Naomi means "pleasant." Naomi asked her village neighbors to call her "Mara," meaning bitter. She said, "The Almighty has dealt very bitterly with me (Ruth 1:20)." Eugene Peterson's *The Message Translation* puts it, "The Strong One has dealt me a bitter blow." Peterson phrases verse 21 as, "I left here full of life, and God has brought me back with nothing but the clothes on my back. Why would you call me Naomi? God certainly doesn't. The Strong One ruined me."

Have you ever felt like that? Have you ever felt no matter what you do there is nothing but defeat? Do you feel even God is set against you? Have you ever felt there were things—powers, personalities, and demonic forces—against you? Perhaps you have felt there were things that seem to run in your family or culture that were not right. They cause continued turmoil, conflict, poverty, and disruption. Demonic personalities are actively engaged in manipulation of people and societies. It is possible they are in yours.

The western world prides itself in science and man's ability to control his destiny. The world of evil, however, is bigger, more widespread and powerful than people recognize. In the flesh, Leviathan is untamable. It cannot be domesticated to accommodate your desires and lifestyle. Demonic powers are impossible to control in the flesh. Salvation and deliverance are the work of God. Deliverance must be by God. Jesus came to destroy the works of the devil and establish the kingdom of God. By faith in him deliverance from the demonic world is possible. It is the portion of all who believe!

People often forsake God and the church. Instead of living the standards of ministry, people make their own rules. They label standards of righteousness and holiness as legalism. Instead of passion for God, they have passion for the world and success. Paul noted that a fellow-laborer, Demas, quit following Christ because he loved this present world. He returned home to Thessalonica (Colossians 4:14; 2 Timothy 4:10). Spiritual appetites become twisted to fleshly and worldly desires. Desires are allowed explosive energy to satisfy the flesh. Things mean everything. People will work extra jobs, overtime, extra days and weekends for whatever it takes to have things.

The twisting nature of Leviathan affects fellowship. It twists relationships. It twists how one views others. It twists how one views the motives and desires of others. Once twisted, they see friends as competitors or even enemies. It is even possible to view leaders as self-serving and arbitrary.

Paul warned the Ephesian elders of this at Miletus. He told them, "I know this, that after my departure savage wolves will come in among you, not sparing the flock. Also, from among yourselves men will rise up, speaking perverse things, to draw away the disciples after themselves (Acts 20:29-30)." Think of this scripture's words. "Savage wolves," Paul says, "will not spare the flock." Who are these "savage wolves?" They were members of congregations who once labored for the sake of the kingdom. They have become twisted, their thinking confused, and their vision dark and demonic. The motives and theologies of other members of the congregation become suspect and are even said at times to be dangerous. Twisted, they leave and seek to draw others to follow them and leave the household of faith.

Under the influence of Leviathan, instead of building the body of Christ, people bite and devour one another. They seek their own preeminence. Instead of building relationships and a fellowship of believers, their words and memories are twisted to personal agendas. They remember things only as they want to remember them. Self-promotion gives little regard to others and destroys church order. Leviathan enflames passions "as from a boiling pot and burning rushes." His breath (the whisper of gossip) "kindles coals" to flame, and a "flame goes out of his mouth (Job 41:20-21)." The powerful emotions of jealousy and envy are enflamed. Much of 2nd Corinthians is Paul's efforts to thwart the drawing away by so-called apostles of disciples to factious divisions.

The force of the twisting spirit of Leviathan impales people in uncertainty, insecurity and paranoia. The impact—personally and corporately—of the demonic assault is visible in churches and in people. Things happen. Some people simply shut down. One pastor of a successful church goes through times that frustrate his pastor. He simply goes "dark." That is, he is out of the picture. He doesn't call, won't answer his phone and apparently does nothing. Like many, his life has not been an easy one. But, he loves God. There are occasions, however, when the rejection of his past or some other event has not been processed properly. He does not see clearly what is happening in his life. His view is focused on an event or situation from the past. It is like he just disappears. He sees no way to move forward or be involved. This is the impact of Leviathan. It is like the mind becomes twisted with the thoughts of "not belonging" or "not belonging in this position" or even "not belonging at all." Maybe it is thoughts like, "I'm not really accomplishing anything," or "I really don't have what it takes to finish." It is like Leviathan has waited for a crucial moment to grasp the mind and begin to twist and tear at it.

Nick Kyrgios is an accomplished tennis player. He is talented, temperamental and capable. He can dominate high level opponents in one match and be destroyed by inferior players the next. In a recent U.S. Open tennis match in Cincinnati he seemed to not even be trying. In his second-round match he moped about the court. Between games he held a towel between his teeth and seemed to want to be anywhere but on the court. He barely lunged for shots, didn't even try to return several serves and was being destroyed. During a changeover the umpire stepped down from his chair and went to where Kyrgios sat and talked with him. There is some controversy about this action. It had, however, the magic of a pep talk and Nick came from behind to beat his opponent to set up a match between himself (number 30 in the world) with Roger Federer, the number three in the world.[4]

Something was happening in Nick's mind. It was reflected in his body language. It changed. The problem was not his ability. Nick Kyrgios had shut down. His attitude was reflected in his performance. It is, perhaps, unlikely that Nick would say it was a demonic assault. It was, however, spiritual. It doesn't just happen to pastors and athletes.

One young woman was talking to a pastor in a hesitant and protective way when suddenly her face became contorted and she burst out with a flood of hateful words against her parents. You occasionally see this in healing crusades. She became physically twisted as she spoke. The hate on the inside became manifest in twisting on the outside. It is like Nebuchadnezzar when the three Hebrew slaves refused to bow down to the golden statue in the plain of Dura. When they refused his command, "He was full of fury, and the expression on his face changed toward Shadrach, Meshach, and Abed-Nego (Daniel 3:19)." Similarly, the demonic twisted this woman physically but had already twisted her mind. A spirit had taken her to the breaking point. She exploded in a rush of hate and bitterness against the parents she had previously claimed were good to her.

Lawlessness is a plague in the world today. It is famously noted that earlier in English history the London police, "Bobbies," carried no weapon. Think of our generation. Police officers today look like they are entering a war zone rather than a neighborhood or community. In many municipalities they carry lethal weapons, less lethal weapons, specialized weapons, body worn cameras and body armor. They carry radios that are connected to national, regional and local information systems. Ten of the fifty largest police departments in the US recently needed double-digit increases in sworn personnel (a 19% increase in Phoenix). In 2012 there were over one million full time police department personnel in the US. There were almost 900,000 sworn officers, or nearly 3 sworn officers per 1000 citizens.[5]

The anti-authority spirit manifests on jobsites, in education, in civil government. People often burst with pent up frustrations—often over things with little value in any current issue. This anti-authority spirit has been on the rise for decades both in the secular world and the church. Anti-authority related occasions occurred in 1990 and again in 2000 in a large fellowship of churches. During one of these "rebellions" a woman member of the church for many years stood and talked of her Christian experience. She mentioned that she wanted to be remembered "not as a great cook, but as a Christian woman." People in the congregation turned to one another and said, "Is she quitting?" Three days later she and her husband told the pastor they were leaving the church. She gave no personal reason. Something twisted in her spirit because of words from people already in rebellion. In fact, she said, "We have nothing against you pastor." Words from people who were already twisted drew her away. The twisting and distorting aspect of Leviathan can be seen in speech and body language at home and at church.

People do not understand many things. What must be understood is this: the demonic powers of Leviathan are set to divide and separate you from one another and to isolate and overpower your life. Leviathan, the powers of darkness, Satan and his demonic spirits desire your soul and will seek to gain it by twisting your mind.

A fatherless generation has a difficult time with rejection and often misinterprets correction and instruction as animosity. At other times correction is understood as being unwanted or even unworthy. An undisciplined mind is a marker of an undisciplined generation. It is difficult to lead or correct such a generation. Separation in the home and especially from a father is a horrible crisis for the human soul.

When Jesus set the parameters for discipleship in John 6 saying, "Unless you eat the flesh of the Son of Man and drink His blood, you have no life in you (John 6:53)," many departed. Basically saying, "No one is going to tell me what to eat and drink!" Really? Are you stupid, ignorant or blind? It is guaranteed—someone, someday will tell you what to do. It may be a jailor, judge, military officer, nurse, doctor, or spouse.

God asked Job if he was able to tame Leviathan. What about you? Have you been able to tame Leviathan? Can you tame Leviathan in the power of your flesh? Have you been able to tame Leviathan in your will or in your emotions? Or do habits, routines, mindsets and behaviors continue to cause you to make bad decisions, violate relationships, cast aside opportunities and squander your livelihood.

The demonic is able to oppress, twist and manipulate human behavior and reactions because people lack dominion. Think about creation. Man and woman were created in the image of God. They were created as sovereigns (rulers) and given dominion over every creature and thing on the earth. The Fall cost humanity what they were created to have—dominion. They have lost their sovereignty over creation and over their own lives.

Paul says, "all have sinned." That is, all have fallen prey to the demonic powers of hell. They have willingly surrendered their sovereignty by giving the powers of darkness a place or opportunity in their lives.

> For you, brethren, have been called to liberty; only do not use liberty as an opportunity [*topos*] for the flesh. (Galatians 5:13)

> "Be angry, and do not sin": do not let the sun go down on your wrath, 27 nor give place [*topos*] to the devil. (Ephesians 4:26-27)

Students of WWII understand that the allies crossed the channel from Great Britain and landed at Normandy, France. There was a tremendous and costly battle to gain a beachhead [a place] on the continent of Europe. Once a beachhead was established the war was virtually decided in the allies' favor. Yes, there were further battles. There were important battles. Nonetheless, with a beachhead they could reinforce the battle with troops and supplies. They could expand their dominion into France and eventually Germany.

The question to ask, personally and corporately, is, "What kind of beachhead in my life has been occupied by the devil?" What place in my/our life has allowed the demonic to establish its rule? What opportunities have been given to the demonic to establish a place in our mind and emotions?

When we are bound to a habit, lust, desire, demonic power, oppression or sin, the question we need to ask is, "What have I surrendered to the demonic world?" "What has made me vulnerable?" We need to ask, "What have I yielded to the devil?" Or, we could instead ask, "What have I not given over to God?"

Has it been a habit? One convert gave a great testimony of deliverance. She was doing really well. But later confessed she never gave up smoking marijuana with "friends." Soon she found herself compromised and began doing all she had been doing before her salvation. Her habit was a beachhead for the demonic. Influence from her friends, the culture of the old life, took over her life again. She lost dominion in her life. Smoking, taking pills to get you up for work and put you to sleep at night, sipping a hot toddy to relax, pornography to relieve the stress, or some other behavior not surrendered to God are all beachheads for demonic assault.

The language you use. Has it been surrendered to God? Or is it the language of the old life, the bitter life? Like Naomi, do you say, "Call me bitter?" Do the frustrations of life overwhelm you? In anger do you tell your spouse, "This marriage is over?" Maybe, like Richard Nixon, you quit saying, "You won't have me to kick around anymore."

The devil is the master of the bold, "Hitleresque," kind of lie. Words and phrases like, "Even if God would intervene it would not be possible for me to serve him." We might say, "It's over for me," or, "There's nothing more to do but quit." During the siege of Samaria, the purser in the gate mocked at even the thought that God could "provide bread in the gate (2 Kings 7:2)." But God did.

The devil boldly asserted to Israel that 1) God has abandoned you, 2) God has divorced you, and 3) God has sold you to his creditors. The people of God repeated the assertion vocally complaining to God. "The Lord has forsaken me, And my Lord has forgotten me (Isaiah 49:14)." We have to be honest here? Israel is saying, "Hey, we are the people of God. How did we end up in Babylon?" Those in denial complain saying they are forsaken and forgotten. Denial says not my fault. Denial says we are entitled to God's blessing. Denial says God is wrong and unfair.

When we yield ourselves to the demonic—when we surrender—we are not merely captured, we are legally possessed by hell because we have broken and/or ignored God's law and will (Isaiah 49:24). Being a lawful captive is perhaps more common than being a victim. Deliverance often depends on giving up the victim and the race mindsets, and the claims of oppression, abuse or a dysfunctional history.

Have you surrendered to the demonic? Have you allowed the demonic to have your spirit, your mind, and/or your thoughts? Has the devil invaded and possessed a beachhead in your desires? Are there desires that are ungodly or untimely? Could it be a desire for a man, or woman, or money, or position? Are you 40-something years old and have disposable time and money? Do you use it to get things "you always wanted, and go places you always wanted to see?"

Do you feel God has abandoned you? Do you feel God has forgotten and even betrayed you? Listen:

> "Can a woman forget her nursing child, And not have compassion on the son of her womb? Surely they may forget, Yet I will not forget you." (Isaiah 49:15)

It's a rhetorical question. It is generally answered in the negative. We are tempted to say, "Certainly not." But we know women do it today. People in every congregation have been deeply wounded by being abandoned—and not just by fathers. The scripture, however, is saying more. God is not given to human passions and desires. He is God—the mighty one of Israel. He is the unchanging God who is the same yesterday, today and forever.

> [Listen again], "See, I have inscribed you on the palms of My hands; Your walls are continually before Me." (Isaiah 49:16)

The payment price for your redemption (the blood of Jesus) is inscribed on his "hands."

The plague of recidivism (the tendency of a convicted criminal to offend again and end up back in prison) is because people believe they are smarter and will not get caught again. They believe they can go back to the old lifestyle and culture without being affected. They believe being imprisoned (a legal captive) was a one-off fluke and won't happen to them again. Pride!

Leviathan is a spirit you must survive. You must survive the whispering of Leviathan in your ear. You must survive Leviathan's strategies and devices. Do you know Leviathan is the king over all the children of pride (Job 41:34)? Pride is the spirit of Lucifer—the spirit of Satan. You will not defeat Leviathan in your pride. Pride says you know better now. Pride says you will never make that mistake again. Pride says I am in control.

When Pastor Campbell committed his life to Christ he was delivered in a moment of time. It happened in a simple prayer. In that moment everything changed. His entire life of addictions, jealousy, rage, his love for fighting and violence changed. That was deliverance. Hell uses arguments, high sounding philosophies and thoughts to establish beachheads within your life. Deliverance frees you from these. When Campbell was saved he was immediately delivered from alcohol. Walking in that deliverance became the habit of his life.

Campbell used to ride motorcycles. His friends came by one day. They said, "Come on, let's go for a ride." Campbell said, "No." They said, "C'mon, just ride along with us." They tried to persuade him. They called out that he didn't have to drink or do anything against his "religion." But Campbell stuck with his "No." Why? Because, he was delivered. Leviathan had been slain. The chains were broken, and the captive had been set free. He was not living that lifestyle any longer. Bikes and rides with the unsaved were not going to be his culture.

Campbell's brother came home from the military and dropped by with some alcohol in hand. Campbell told him, "You're welcome and can come in but," pointing to the alcohol, "that isn't coming in." His brother became angry and challenged him. He said Joe didn't appreciate all he had done for him. Indeed his older brother had done many things for him. He took him to games, bought him his first baseball glove and helped him in numerous ways. Campbell, however, did not want his old life to come back in his home. He was changed. Leviathan had been pierced through with God's sword. Campbell's brother was a brilliant person and soldier. But he was an alcoholic who died with a half-empty bottle beside his bed. God had taken his sword and destroyed the power of Leviathan in Campbell's life.

Never underestimate the power of salvation. It is the power of a new life. When a soul is saved, born-again, and delivered from sin it is a work of God. It is a work of God that defeats the powers of hell and darkness. The power of God frees from bondages, habits, evil thoughts and sin. Salvation is the great miracle of the kingdom of God. It is the power of God made manifest in and through humanity. It is the great promise of God. It is God's great joy. The slaying of Leviathan is by God's design and his great power.

> Shall the prey be taken from the mighty, or the lawful captives be delivered? 25 But thus saith Jehovah, Even the captives of the mighty shall be taken away, and the prey of the terrible shall be delivered; for I will contend with him that contendeth with thee, and I will save thy children. ... and all flesh shall know that I, Jehovah, am thy Saviour, and thy Redeemer, the Mighty One of Jacob. (Isaiah 49:24-26 ASV)

This is the very reason for Jesus leaving the glory of heaven and coming to us as a man.

> He who sins is of the devil, for the devil has sinned from the beginning. For this purpose the Son of God was manifested, that He might destroy the works of the devil. (1 John 3:8)

Even the lawful captive can be delivered from the powers of darkness. It is the promise of God. Exodus 12:13 gives us the Old Testament truth.

> "Now the blood shall be a sign for you on the houses where you are. And when I see the blood, I will pass over you; and the plague shall not be on you to destroy you when I strike the land of Egypt."

This truth is memorialized in the Passover meal and unleavened bread eaten by devout Jews. God, in the victory of Jesus, is doing a new thing.

Jacquelle Crowe, as a teen, wrote a book for teens about the miracle of salvation. In it she tells the story of a prominent pastor. He heard a message at a youth conference that stunned him. The speaker said being a Christian wouldn't change anything. You could keep the same friends and keep up the same activities. In effect, the things you enjoyed would remain things you could enjoy even after salvation. She titled her book, *This Changes Everything.* She then went on to explain salvation meant friendships and relationships were all changed. The view of God and the church were changed. Salvation changed everything. Jesus, through the Holy Spirit transformed everything about her life. In a moment of time and through a simple prayer everything changed.[6]

Exodus records the great deliverance of Israel from Pharaoh's power and the destruction of the Egyptian Army.

> But the children of Israel had walked on dry land in the midst of the sea, and the waters were a wall to them on their right hand and on their left. So the Lord saved Israel that day out of the hand of the Egyptians, and Israel saw the Egyptians dead on the seashore. Thus Israel saw the great work which the Lord had done in Egypt; so the people feared the Lord, and believed the Lord and His servant Moses. (Exodus 14:29-31)

Think of it. The last plague in Egypt proved God's power over life and death. The resurrection of Jesus from the dead again proved God's power over life and death. When the Hebrew's cry of affliction rose to God, he raised a deliverer. But it was God's power. It was not the power of Moses or Aaron that brought deliverance. God delivered them by his power and his might. God did something no man could do. God defeated and brought Pharaoh to his knees. Jesus defeated death, hell and the grave.

The Apostle John writes of the power of God and the overthrow of the powers of darkness in Revelation.

> Then I heard a loud voice saying in heaven, "Now salvation, and strength, and the kingdom of our God, and the power of His Christ have come, for the accuser of our brethren, who accused them before our God day and night, has been cast down. 11 And they overcame him by the blood of the Lamb and by the word of their testimony. (Revelation 12:10-11)

Deliverance for Israel was by the blood of the Passover lamb and the power of God. Today deliverance is still by the blood of Jesus Christ (the Passover Lamb) and Power of God. Jesus is the sinless Lamb of God whose vicarious suffering and death paid the price for our deliverance from the jaws of hell.

The believer's life is a life of faith. It is not just any faith but faith in God. Paul notes the inability to do, in the flesh, all that we might desire to do.

> I find then a law, that evil is present with me, the one who wills to do good. 22 For I delight in the law of God according to the inward man. 23 But I see another law in my members, warring against the law of my mind, and bringing me into captivity to the law of sin which is in my members. 24 O wretched man that I am! Who will deliver me from this body of death? 25 I thank God—through Jesus Christ our Lord! (Romans 7:21-25)

Time and occasion are important to your behavior and how it is interpreted. At the end of the book of Job, God began to confront him over the issue of Leviathan. What are you going to do with this spirit?

Are you going to make a covenant with it? Are you going hire it to do service for you? What are you going to do, Job? Are you going to make a decision? When the events of your life do not square with your plans or ideas, how are you going to go forward?

Another way to say it is, "What you see is *not* all there is." In other words, decisions are often based on what we see. Such decisions can, and often do, lead to tragedy. What Hebrews points out is that what you see is "NOT" all there is. The worlds were made by God. Hence decisions made based on only what you see can often be wrong.

The things that are made are not made of what they seem. This is a powerful reality when it comes to deliverance from the Satanic, the demonic, sin and pride.

> By faith we understand that the worlds were framed by the word of God, so that the things which are seen were not made of things which are visible (Hebrews 11:3).

This understanding gave rise to the question, "I wonder," the two pastors said, "How many things are spiritual." How much is the result of things unseen. How many things get in our heads because of thinking we see or know everything. It would be amusing were not often tragic to hear people defending their decisions saying, "I know a few things!" Perhaps the word "few" should be the emphasis.

Jesus, at the Last Supper, was asked what he meant when he said someone would betray him. Jesus said, "I tell you the truth, one of you will betray me." The disciples, "Greatly distressed," each one asked in turn, "Am I the one, Lord?"

We can also ask, "Am I the one?" Good question. Are you, the one listening to the deceit of Leviathan? Are you thinking there is nothing happening in the kingdom, or nothing in it for you? Are you the one thinking the family is destroyed, the marriage is over, the ministry is done, or this is the worst my life has ever been?

Are you hearing what the Word of God says, give no "place" or opportunity to the devil? You might say, "What is that about?" I don't have any idols in my house! Really? No idols in your mind? No places in your spirit or heart that are strongholds of attitudes, hurts, rejections or offenses (grudges) giving a place for the demonic to take advantage of you?

At one point, Jesus said to Peter, "Get behind me, Satan." That is, "get in line." When we get in line with God it releases his sword. When we get in line by obedience the sword of the Lord is unsheathed for deliverance. When we get in line with God's words rather than ours we release God to save and set free. When we get in line by repenting, God forgives and redeems. When God unsheathes his sword there is deliverance. God's sword is the weapon that slays Leviathan.

Do you know what the umpire said to Nick Kyrgios? "He said, 'I know you. I know how good you are. This doesn't look good.'" In other words, "You are making tennis look bad." Do you make Jesus look bad? Does your life make you look bad? Does your Christian life make God and Jesus look bad? Is your life filled with sin? Is it filled with perversions and the demonic? Do you hate the way you are living and dealing with people? Do you need deliverance? "Isaiah says, "even the lawful captive" can be set free.

Joseph C. Campbell and John W. Gooding

CHAPTER 2

THE NECESSARY DISTINCTION

Surely, I spoke of things ... too wonderful for me to know (Job 42:3)

Shortly after preaching on Leviathan, that twisting serpent (*I Hear Those Chains Falling*), Pastor Campbell received a phone call. It was from a pastor in California. The pastor said he appreciated the sermon and understood about deliverance. But, he continued, "What happens when people who have experienced powerful deliverance and have lived powerfully for God turn back to the old life?" Sometimes, he went on, it is after a short while. Some people, however, have lived for God two, five, or even ten years and then turn back to the old life and the world.

"Something happened when this pastor called me." Campbell said, "It was like suddenly the penny dropped. It became a revelation to me." He could relate to what this pastor was saying. Campbell said you can read the Bible, but it's different when it becomes a revelation. "It was like things I knew and had pondered for years. They suddenly dropped into place in my soul and spirit. The reality of dominion became more real than gravity to me." Campbell continued, "Revelation will change your world."

Deliverance is not dominion. "I remembered a beautifully delivered soul who went back to the streets and drugs after having a testimony and living for God ten years." She had been delivered from an injustice that could have ruined her life. She was blessed and helped by friends and family to set up a lifestyle that God blessed. She was a marvelous testimony of the life God could give someone terribly ruined by the "system" and by her street life of self-destruction. Deliverance will take you out of Egypt. Deliverance will take you off the streets. Deliverance will take you out of the bars and set you free from alcohol. Deliverance will set you free from drugs, lusts, perversion and violence. But, deliverance is not dominion.

Deliverance is something God does. It is by the blood of the Lamb (Jesus) and the power of God. Israel was delivered by the supernatural power of God. The blood of Jesus and the power of God delivered this young woman. She was set free from the self-destruction of the streets. She was delivered from condemnation and her rage against life. Deliverance will set you free. But deliverance does not automatically compute out as dominion. Deliverance got the Israelites out of Egypt but it did not deposit them in the Promised Land. Dominion will take you to the Promised Land. Dominion will take you to your destiny and the blessing of God.

In deliverance, God does the heavy lifting. God heard the cry of the Israelites in Egypt. He reached down from heaven with miracle power and delivered them. God empowered Moses and Aaron to confront and face down Pharaoh. They confronted Pharaoh time and again until finally Pharaoh said, "Go." After leaving Egypt, Israel faced the Red Sea. Israel crossed the Red Sea. They crossed on dry ground. Pharaoh and his army tried to recapture the people of God. They tried to cross the sea as God's people did. God, however, caused the waters to flow back and close the path. Israel saw Pharaoh's army drown in the waters of the sea. Pharaoh's army perished.

When Israel was free from Pharaoh they came to the wilderness. They came to a place where they had to walk in their freedom. In one of the great tragedies of history all but two of those thousands and thousands who came out of Egypt died in the wilderness. In the first census after being delivered Moses numbered six hundred thousand five-hundred-and-fifty men over twenty and available for battle (Numbers 3:32). They all, except two, failed to enter the Promised Land.

They failed to possess the destiny and inheritance God had prepared for them. They were delivered but they had no dominion.

Israel, they sang, they danced, and they rejoiced after crossing the sea. But they had no experience in the wilderness. They had been slaves in Egypt. Slavery was all they knew. They did not know faith and dominion. It was not their power that delivered them. It was God's power. The only power they had ever known before was the power of muscle for making bricks and fighting. They knew only the oppressive power of taskmasters.

Deliverance is what God does. Deliverance is what frees the soul from the bondage of Egypt—the world and sin. Deliverance is what frees one's soul from the twisting spirit of Leviathan. Deliverance is what sets the soul free from the passions that rage against circumstances, people and existence. In deliverance, it is God who does the miraculous. It is not by our might, our wisdom, or our power. Deliverance is by the power and will of God.

Dominion is when you walk in the reality of deliverance. Dominion is when you frame your world by faith in God. Dominion is when you order your life in the word of God. Dominion is when you walk in obedience to God by faith. Dominion is when 2nd Corinthians 10 becomes a reality in your mind and life.

> For though we walk in the flesh, we do not war according to the flesh. 4 For the weapons of our warfare are not carnal but mighty in God for pulling down strongholds, 5 casting down arguments and every high thing that exalts itself against the knowledge of God, bringing every thought into captivity to the obedience of Christ, 6 and being ready to punish all disobedience when your obedience is fulfilled. (2 Corinthians 10:3-6)

Dominion is when you pull down strongholds. Dominion is when you cast down arguments and things that rise in opposition to God and the knowledge (truth) of God. Demonic personalities or spirits gain access and establish their dominions as strongholds. These demonic powers exercise rule in your life. The demonic gains a place of rule through repetitive sin, persistent attitudes, and wrongful and even unwitting influence from others. When you are pulling down the strongholds of your past you are walking in dominion.

You walk in dominion when you are casting down arguments that resist God and God's will in your life. They can be high-sounding arguments from the realm of philosophy, reason or religion. These are offered as excuses for continued sinfulness or disobedience to God. You walk in dominion when you take captive thoughts that oppose obedience to God. When you do not let your mind run wild in suspicions, suppositions, and falsehoods you are walking in dominion.

When Pastor Campbell committed his life to Christ he was delivered in a moment of time. Dominion came when he began to make decisions. Deliverance frees you. Nonetheless, there are long held patterns of living that do not automatically drop off. When he refused to ride with the old friends and participate in the old culture dominion began to grow in his life. When he refused his brother's alcohol it caused a big argument. The decision to keep alcohol out of his house was a step into dominion and destiny.

Dominion is established by choices. Your will and your mind are intimately connected. You'll become crazy if you try to separate them. When you make a choice in your mind your will must follow that choice. Similarly, when you set your will your mind must follow. When you decide or set your will to be a Christian and live as a Christian in obedience then you establish a culture of dominion.

Dominion is a way of thinking. It is established in the way you think about the affairs and events of life. It is a way of thinking that cast down the strongholds, thoughts and arguments of the old life and the cultures of the world. How you think when you experience failure determines your dominion. How you think about disappointments in life establishes dominion or its loss. The culture of your soul in dominion becomes God's arena. Or, without dominion it can be an avenue for the demonic. What happens in your mind when temptation strikes? What happens in your mind when the unexpected or unfamiliar come into your life? What happens in your mind when the marriage struggles, or the kids go another direction?

Events—especially crises—are the arenas where demonic personalities and powers derail your deliverance. Pharaoh told Moses and the Israelites they could go but changed his mind. So also, the demonic seeks to regain control over you. In a crisis you can cave in to a "pity-party," a "poor-me attitude," or "what's the use" mindset, and backslide. You can even become seven-times worse. Many have seen it happen.

It is important to know and understand that deliverance does not automatically mean dominion. It is also important to know that you can have dominion in one area and not have it in another. Because you experience dominion in one area does not mean you have dominion in every area of your life.

Deliverance is the work of a moment. It is a miracle. All that is involved is a simple prayer. It is a cry to God for help to escape the oppression of hell. It is simple enough, but in that moment everything changes. Some people never touch or taste another drop of alcohol. Some people never drop another hit of acid, take pills, get high, or smoke another joint. Many establish order in their broken marriage and raise a successful family. Deliverance dramatically changes attitudes and worldviews. The possibilities of God's power are endless.

Think about it. You can be delivered, and powerfully so. Without dominion, however, you will fail, quit or go back to your old life. Dominion is how you possess destiny and the promises of God. What is dominion? It is where you rule over your decisions. It is when and where you exercise sovereignty in the arena of your life. Dominion is what you were created to possess as a free moral agent with choice.

The spiritual life depends on deliverance. You must be born again. But many other things lay hold of us in life. Dallas Willard says, "We pick up beliefs like a coat picks up lint."[1] Deliverance and deliverances are all the work of God and his power, but dominion has to do with your walk following deliverance.

God framed the world for faith. Faith is God's frame for the picture you make of your life. Faith must be the story-line of the life you live. Faith must be the boundary or border that encases all that is allowed in our life. Faith, however, is not religion.

In America and the Western world today religion comes from many sources. It comes from Hinduism, Islam, Buddhism and other ideas mixed with Christianity. Charles Kraft has noted in *Christianity with Power*:

> It is interesting (and discouraging) to note that even though we are Christians, our basic assumptions are usually more like those of the non-Christian Westerners around us than we would like to admit.... [W]e often find ourselves more Western than scriptural.[2]

Western Christianity has been through the enlightenment, the scientific and industrial revolutions and adopted a materialistic worldview. Today western Christianity is nothing like New Testament Christianity.

It had always been true that there was an understanding of accountability in life and in the life to come. The basic understanding of accountability has gone missing. As David Wells says, today's generation is in a unique moment trying to build a civilization without a religious foundation. David Wells in *Courage to be Protestant* says, it is building a civilization of "ingenuity and intricacy." Today's Christian is often building a life of materialism that does not provide a frame for understanding this life or the life to come. There is no place for faith, no place for morality, no place for a Lord and savior. However, Wells says, in one way or another you will frame your life by what is of ultimate importance and value to you. Dominion must be framed by faith and the lordship of Jesus the Christ.

The work of salvation and deliverance is a work of God. It is God who changes us. Jesus changed Simon's Peter's name from a pebble to a stone. Jacob's name was changed from a conniving mommy's boy to a Prince with God. Jabez' life was transformed when he called on God from a sorrowful beginning he became "more honorable than his brethren (1 Chronicles 4:9)." Jesus even gives a new name to overcomers (Revelation 2:17). The inner transformation is a work of God.

Faith and unbelief describe how you process the events of your life. Faith marks out the lines in pleasant places (Psalms 16:6) for a believer's life. "By faith we understand that the worlds were framed by the word of God, so that the things which are seen were not made of things which are visible (Hebrews 11:3)." God has framed the world. That is, he has given it a structure that accommodates faith.

Life can be processed in many ways. It can be processed in anger, in the old lifestyle, in the culture of your family, friends and/or peers. It can be processed in a spiritual but non-christian way. It can be processed in numb denial. Only faith in Jesus brings about dominion. This is what gives structure and meaning to life.

When Paul was imprisoned in Philippi, where had preached the gospel, and the first European convert to Christ (Lydia) was saved and a demon possessed girl delivered, it created an uproar in the city. Paul and Silas were unjustly thrown into prison. There are many ways to understand events like these. Paul chose to frame these events by faith in Christ.

> But I want you to know, brethren, that the things which happened to me have actually turned out for the furtherance of the gospel (Philippians 1:12)

Paul writes to tell the brethren that what they can see, his chains, is not the whole story. He continues: it is "evident to the whole palace guard, and to all the rest, that my chains are in Christ (Philippians 1:13)." Paul framed his chains in faith. He also framed injustice and setbacks in Christ's purposes and calling. This makes all the difference. As you read the story, Paul and Silas, are not without dominion. They are imprisoned in a dark damp cave that served as a prison in Philippi. But, they are singing and praising God. And God delivered them, with a great deliverance. It resulted in the salvation of an entire household. What happens to you when injustice and setbacks happen?

Framing the events of life in Christ is powerful. It establishes dominion. When events are framed outside of faith they become avenues for demonic assault and loss of dominion. If you frame events as injustices, they become strongholds. They become the controlling issues in the mind. They can be manipulated by demonic personalities and forces.

When you process the events of life repeatedly using the same negative formulas—it's always going to be this way, it always happens to me, no one cares, I'll never be adequate, I don't see how any good thing can come out of this event, God's unfair, and poor me—the brain bundles nerve pathways together forming a natural channel of thinking and a strong mental barrier to change. These mental pathways divert God's plan. His power, deliverance and dominion are limited.

Abigail was the wife of Nabal. He was a worthless, ungodly man. He rejected David's protection of his herds and flocks. He denied that David had helped him and rudely declined to reward David's men for their efforts. David understood the protection of this man's flocks and herds had been in vain. David prepared himself and his men to destroy Nabal and his household. David framed this affront as a warrior would. Nabal's wife, Abigail, hastened to meet David before his men destroyed her household. She came to David with a word from God. She was able to change David's reference point and reframe his situation with an inspired word. She put a frame of faith and God's plan around the events of David's life. Abigail said to David:

> Now therefore, my lord, as the Lord lives and as your soul lives, since the Lord has held you back from coming to bloodshed and from avenging yourself with your own hand, now then, let your enemies and those who seek harm for my lord be as Nabal. (1 Samuel 25:26)

> For the Lord will certainly make for my lord an enduring house, because my lord fights the battles of the Lord, and evil is not found in you throughout your days. 29 Yet a man has risen to pursue you and seek your life, but the life of my lord shall be bound in the bundle of the living with the Lord your God; and the lives of your enemies He shall sling out, as from the pocket of a sling. 30 And it shall come to pass, when the Lord has done for my lord according to all the good that He has spoken concerning you, and has appointed you ruler over Israel, 31 that this will be no grief to you, nor offense of heart to my lord, either that you have shed blood without cause, or that my lord has avenged himself. But when the Lord has dealt well with my lord, then remember your maidservant." (1 Samuel 25:28-31)

Abigail successfully and prophetically not only reframed David's life in faith but also her own. David's original frame of reference was from his culture as a warrior. He sought immediate justice. Abigail brought him to understand his life must be framed together with the purposes and plan of God. It was a plan involving not just David but all of Israel. Abigail reframed her life as dependent on God rather than the "scoundrel" and "fool" Nabal. She framed David's life by noting that wanton vengeance would go badly for his reputation and future. Many do not frame their life with the plan of God in mind. Often people do not frame their life with a view to the future. Those who look only at the short term and immediate often spoil their future. They thwart what God would do for them.

God delivered the Hebrews from Egypt. God has delivered countless people throughout the ages from sin. God delivers out of sin's slavery. Israel stood on the far shore of the Red Sea and sang songs of victory. They sang of Pharaoh's Army, his chariots and horses being drowned in the sea. They danced and rejoiced. There was great joy.

But it was only hours until they were confronted by *"life."* The circumstances changed. They came to a bitter place. When the circumstances changed they fell back on their old mindsets and behaviors. Institutionalized cultural behavior took over. For the Jews, their 430 years of slavery had programmed their mind to think certain ways. They, like they did back in Egypt, began to grumble and complain. Like all slaves did when they faced difficulties.

The believer's life, however, is a life of faith. It is not just any faith, but faith in the Creator God. The cultural reactions and thought processes of your past are strongholds and are not adequate for life. They are not adequate for processing calamities and disasters. Over time they became your normal approach to life. While we were sinners, they were our worldview. Habits of thinking were reinforced by experiences. They were reinforced by opinions and attitudes of those around us. They became mental strongholds. "Once an addict, always an addict," is a cultural stronghold of the drug world. "Once an alcoholic, always an alcoholic," is the stronghold of the alcoholic's world. It is a fashionable slogan for those bound by alcohol. They say, "I am a recovering alcoholic." It is never a deliverance or freedom from alcohol. It is always an alcoholic still in bondage.

When we step out of a surrendered relationship with God—out from under his Lordship—we step away from dominion. When the things of the world gain preeminence, our lives move away from dominion. Paul writes tellingly of a former colleague who abandoned him saying, "[He] has forsaken me, having loved this present world, and has departed … (1 Timothy 4:10)." Paul saw the affections of the world had cost his colleague spiritual dominion.

Daniel knew the king's delicacies, Babylonian religion, and idolatry were incompatible with dominion. What are the delicacies of the modern world? Position and status? Toys? Games of fantasy? Indulgences and other time wasters?

There are things that must be resisted. Some things are not conducive to dominion. Peer pressure, fear of separation from friends and family, and fear of rejection must be resisted. To be under the Lordship of Jesus one must resist the temptation to quit or run away when things do not go as expected. Fleshly desires are incompatible for deliverance. Doubt is incompatible for deliverance. The issue is "how you process the events that transpire in your life."

Dave Marks pastors a church in Chilliwack, British Columbia. It is not far from Vancouver. Canada has a large welfare budget that serves thousands of people. For the fiscal year ending March 31, 2014 Canada's federal government spent $276.8 billion on welfare. That represents roughly 15 per cent of Canada's $1.9 trillion economy. The Canadian Institute for Health Information (CIHI) believes Canada spent approximately $228 billion on health care in 2016. That's 11.1 per cent of Canada's entire GDP or $6,299 for every Canadian resident. With monies transferred from the national treasuries to the provinces probably around 15–20% of the federal budget goes to "welfare" programs. Yet, there remains a large homeless population.

When Dave meets the homeless on the street or when they come into his church he asks them, "What's your story?" In other words, he's asking how they became homeless or destitute. The theme of their story is usually an event that turned their world upside down. Many were not saved or born-again when something happened and their life came crashing down around them. Some were from good homes and good parents. Others were already in difficult but functional situations. Then something happened. A storm of life hit. It knocked them down. It could have been a divorce, lost job, death of a spouse or child, self-destructive behaviors of drug abuse and alcoholism and even imprisonment. What Pastor Marks discovered from their stories is common. Life became uncertain. They were unable to move ahead.

Things changed, and it was like everything became difficult. Circumstances became perplexing. Often, they might say they could not understand what or why things happened the way they did. The common denominator in most of these stories is an inability to process life's events. Whatever the event, it became the defining moment of their lives. Everything from that point forward was filtered through the one defining moment. Life stopped. They were unable to take the steps or actions necessary to move forward.

For Israel, the events of the wilderness did not fit their experience. They did not match their worldview. As slaves everything was either done to them or done for them. In the wilderness they would have to walk. Their slave view of life and expectations shaped how they would act and respond to the wilderness. After their deliverance they would have to deal with thirst, bitterness, enemies, the demonic, curses and temptation. Their way to fix things as slaves was to complain, murmur, and plot against their taskmasters. It was all they knew as slaves. On their wilderness journey, just like in Egypt, every crisis was met with complaint, murmuring and anger against Moses. Deliverance had changed their whole world, but they did not know how to process their new life. It was unfamiliar, uncertain and complex.

Think about these people. They were slaves for over 400 years. They were held in bondage physically, economically, socially and spiritually. They became an institutionalized culture. Slavery was a culture they knew and understood. Freedom and liberty was new. They needed God's deliverance from slavery. This was accomplished overnight by the power of God. Four hundred and thirty years of experience was overturned in a night. In deliverance God can overturn a lifetime of rebellion, iniquity and insane behavior.

Moses and Aaron faced Pharaoh and told him, "The Lord God," says, "Let my people go." The Hebrew slaves were the core of Pharaoh's economy and empire building. Pharaoh refused. Pharaoh said, "No." The slavery continued and became more oppressive. God sent a series of ten plagues. God's power was revealed. It was not a demonstration of human or fleshly strength. Ten plagues from God engulfed Egypt and Pharaoh. The plagues began when the Nile River—the source of Egypt's livelihood—was turned to blood. The second plague was frogs that filled the rivers, houses, and even the beds of the Egyptians. Following Pharaoh's continuing refusal plagues of lice, flies and livestock disease came on the Egyptians. Further plagues troubled Egypt but spared where the Hebrews lived in Goshen. This was a dramatic demonstration of God's power over the events of life. A sixth plague, boils, struck even the demonized magicians that resisted God. The boils came on man and beast but not on the Hebrews or their livestock. Hail, locust and darkness were the seventh, eighth, and ninth plagues. The plague of darkness struck the heart of Egyptian worship. The sun god, Ra, was shut out. The final plague was the death of the firstborn.

These plagues were a manifestation of God's power. Christianity is a religion of revelation. God reveals himself in power. John Newton said, "If you see the ark of God falling (picturing the story of moving the Ark of the Covenant up to Jerusalem in 2 Samuel 6), you can be quite sure that it is due to a swimming in your head."[3] In other words, God has not changed. He has not become incapable doing whatever he desires. God has not and will not "fall or fail" from his pedestal as did Dagon, the Philistine god. God has the power to accomplish his purposes. Repeatedly Moses spoke the same words to Pharaoh. It was a simple two phrases. First Moses said to Pharaoh, "Let my people go," then he said, "That they may serve me."

There can be a lot of swimming in one's head that does not lead to fruitfulness and productivity. There is purpose in deliverance. It is not just freedom for the sake of freedom. God has a desire to dwell with his people and for them to dwell with him.

In the uncertainty of the wilderness Israel began to fantasize. Their thought life became occupied with life back in Egypt. Like many people facing hardships they fantasize about how life used to be. One young man complained about his "Christian" girlfriend saying, his sinner girlfriend treated him better. Of course, it's possible that his new girlfriend wasn't all that Christian either. And, then again, maybe it was just him! Fantasies about old girlfriends, boyfriends, about good times and memories can crowd out reality and obscure the path to destiny. Mockingly, the Israelites said, "What's this (manna)?" They were fantasizing about leeks and garlics like they were a prime rib dinner.

A friend of the poor soul that went back to the world after ten years of Christian life was asked, "How did that happen?" The response was enlightening. "[She] never cut loose the old life." She found it easy to maintain and understand the old familiar life. The old life is what she knew and understood. She knew the codes of conduct, the surroundings were familiar, and there were images of the "good-old' times." She kept track of old friends. She followed their lives and stories. Perhaps she fantasized about what might have been or could still be. Some people look up their old relationships. In their minds they establish a fantasy life. They put together fanciful scenarios forgetting the consequences that had put the chains of bondage on their necks in the past.

Overshadowing our reactions to the events of life is our worldview. It comes primarily from our culture. We react according to the culture we are familiar with. The familiar culture of Israel was slavery. It was all they knew. We pick up the clues of how to process life from our culture. David Wells is the distinguished research professor at Gordon-Conwell Theological Seminary. Wells says, "Our social context, to put it formally, powerfully shapes our internal consciousness." Our culture is a powerful component in how we process meaning in events. Our social context (culture) is a large factor in the reactions and thoughts we have when things change in our external world.

We are products of the world we live in. Yes, there is a DNA component in life. Yes, there are issues in your nature and physical being. But there is no question that your culture plays a profound role in how you live and cope with life. You have heard it said, "You are what you eat." Similarly, you are what your culture is. Israel needed deliverance. God "brought them up out of the land of Egypt." The slave culture dominated their reactions to the wilderness life.

Russell Moore's *The Storm-Tossed Family*[4] notes the central place family plays in our lives.

> We not only learn who we are; we often gain an inheritance through the family. We gain patterns of life, expectations, models, and wounds from our family of origin. Our life stories show us that we are part of a larger story—a story brimming with other characters.

> No matter how much we want to believe that we have shaped and formed ourselves, that we control our own personality and destiny, we all come from somewhere, and more to the point, from some people. (38-39)

Family is a primary source of our identity and our inheritance You can leave home and never see or deal with your relatives again. You can make deliberate choices to change religion, political party and career. You can make yourself as different as possible but when you look in the mirror you still see features of your father and mother. When you argue or deliver a speech you will hear things your father and mother said to you. In the training ground of your family it is possible you learned a distortion of your identity or inheritance. Moore says you may have learned you would never amount to anything. You may have learned you are a mere tool or extension of your parents. You may have picked up and been molded with a bent to depression, or picked up an addiction, or learned a system of living in strife and trauma. Family could have left you with limited resources or social skills.

It's hard to imagine a family with more dysfunction than the one where a band of brothers beat their younger sibling nearly to death in a jealous rage. As the youngster approached death one of the brothers talked the others into selling him in a human trafficking scheme (Moore, 40). Many know the story of Joseph. Andrew Lloyd Weber made it a musical—*Joseph and the Amazing Technicolor Dreamcoat*. An essential part of who you are is the story of where you came from.

The power of family to shape lives is part of the New Testament story. How far and how wide does culture reach? Jesus scathing rebuke of the Scribes and Pharisees ends with the statement that "they are just like those" who murdered the prophets.

> [You say] 'If we had lived in the days of our fathers, we would not have been partakers with them in the blood of the prophets.' 31 "Therefore you are witnesses against yourselves that you are sons of those who murdered the prophets. 32 Fill up, then, the measure of your fathers' guilt.... that on you may come all the righteous blood shed on the earth, from the blood of righteous Abel to the blood of

> Zechariah, son of Berechiah, whom you murdered between the temple and the altar. (Matthew 23:30-36)

Stephen, the first martyr, repeated the same accusation.

> You stiff-necked and uncircumcised in heart and ears! You always resist the Holy Spirit; as your fathers did, so do you. (Acts 7:51)

Do you see the importance of the statement, "as your fathers?" Jesus and Stephen reach back generations for the source of the "murderous instinct." The pull of generational curses and behaviors reaches through many generations. Over five-hundred years had passed since Zechariah was murdered and over four-hundred years since Malachi had preached, and the Jews still wanted to kill the prophet in their midst.

When Paul ministered to the gentiles, he admonished them to, "no longer walk as the rest of the Gentiles walk, in the futility of their mind (Ephesians 4:17)." That is, don't walk as your pagan fathers walked. Don't walk as your culture has walked.

When the Jews crossed over the Red Sea they had been slaves for generations. It was a culture that had a long reach. It cost them dominion and their promised inheritance. It didn't, however, have to cost them.

> You must unlearn old patterns and models. Yes. Are you therefore hopeless? Are you predestined to repeat the disappointments or traumas enacted upon you? By no means. Your inheritance is not just your future reward in the world to come. Your inheritance is also a new Spirit and a new community, able to overcome through you all the snares of the Evil One. (Moore, 42)

Israel would have to unlearn the culture of slavery. They would have to learn new ways to relate to authority. Especially important was learning to deal with discipline. Discipline is the heart of discipleship. It has long been understood that how one reacts to discipline or correction tells a lot about the heart of a person. Israel would have to learn the art of leadership and submission. They would have to learn that love and lust were not the same thing. They would have to learn how to worship God and love their neighbor. They would have to learn how to handle life when it did not go their way. They would have to learn how to handle difficulties, setbacks and perplexing situations. They would have to unlearn the ways they had always handled life. Generally, they had settled difficulties by fighting or quitting.

It is interesting during the Viet Nam era in America, judges would have to deal with incorrigible young men. Often, they would offer them a choice—would you like to go to prison or would you like to join the military? Often, they chose the military where they would have to unlearn the old culture of rebellion and become loyal to a military unit and its leader.

The consequences of family life can be many. Parents must be careful to not assume—that if you remain unmarried, remain unemployed and do not earn a living, live in alcoholism or drug addictions, remain emotionally harsh and abusive—that there will be no impact on your children ... grandchildren and their grandchildren. Snares and offenses come on everyone. Moore says parents should be careful that they are not the cause of the offenses that come on their children (42).

The real danger is that we do not see our cultural inheritance for what it is. It is true that many abandoned children grow up to abandon their own families. It is true that many children of alcoholic families grow up to be alcoholics. And it is true that children from violent homes grow up to reproduce violent homes. These things are true. Not for all. Often, however, it is because they do not recognize their own vulnerability. Some people consistently deny their childhood difficulties painting a picture of a model childhood. They do not see how vulnerable they are to the reach of their culture.

Of course, the dominant culture of the world is sin. We know and see it all the time—and we may even see it in ourselves. One sin, one moral lapse leads to another. Sin is remarkably able to produce more sin. In the common scenario the one sin triggers the next—or the present sin has been triggered by the previous sin.[5]

This is the impact of Psalms 1. Evil and good are contrasted in the Psalm—both, however, have great reproductive capacity. Evil shows up in corrupt families that produce more corrupt families. The abusive home produces more abusive homes.

> Blessed is the man / Who walks not in the counsel of the ungodly, / Nor stands in the path of sinners, / Nor sits in the seat of the scornful; / 2 But his delight is in the law of the Lord, / And in His law he meditates day and night. / 3 He shall be like a tree / Planted by the rivers of water, / That brings forth its fruit in its season, / Whose leaf also shall not wither; / And whatever he does shall prosper. (Psalm 1:1-3)

The good and the bad both bring forth an abundance of their kind. The wild tree produces as does the good tree. It is important to understand sin. Augustine says,

> Our nature was already present in the seed from which we were to spring. And because of this nature has been soiled and justly condemned, no man to be born in any other condition. Thus, from a bad use of free choice, a sequence of misfortunes conducts the whole human race, excepting those redeemed by the grace of God, from the original canker in its root to the devastation of a second and endless death.

We know what wisdom has taught for generations, "People rarely commit single sins." Why do people sin? What is the cause? What is the solution? Some say it is the quest for security—but we all still depend on the provident hand of God. Others say it is unbelief because we refuse to trust and count on the goodness of God.

Woody Allen was close when asked about his affair with the daughter of his wife, Mia Farrow. "The heart wants what it wants."

That's a conversation stopper! "The heart wants what it wants."

The news is filled with the grossest of sins. People form study groups and colleges and universities give courses in the social dynamics of cultures. But you will rarely hear the issue called sin! "The heart wants what it wants."

> The heart is deceitful above all things, And desperately wicked; Who can know it? 10 I, the Lord, search the heart, I test the mind, Even to give every man according to his ways, According to the fruit of his doings. (Jeremiah 17:9-10)

Arthur Koestler was a German author who joined the German Communist Party in 1931. He resigned in 1938 over the atrocities of Stalinism. The one time defender of communism wrote a novel, *Darkness at Noon*, as a critique of communism.

What distressed Koestler the most was the absence of blame. Blame disappeared. Nobody blamed the reluctant or demonstrating peasant who lost their land and livelihood, nobody blamed the critics of the party line or party agenda. Instead, those in power offered pity and reeducation. Pity made the mental institution the place of deliverance for ignorance and the concentration camp the place for reeducation of critics. But no one was blamed. It was, Koestler thought, the end of society. Persons who are not blamed are not held responsible. They are not responsible for their own behavior. They are not considered human—at least not fully so. They are objects to be manipulated for the convenience of the state. The impact was, for Koestler, no one was held accountable. When no one is accountable, then any form of society fails.[6]

Society flounders because it will not call sin, sin. Instead society throws money and more money at things that will not help. Alcoholism treated as a disease impinges on the health care system. Money is spent on the search for "cures" when the issue is, "the heart wants what it wants." There are many other things we do not want to call sin!

> I said, "You are gods, And all of you are children of the Most High." (Psalm 82:6)

That is, we are made as sovereigns over our own lives. We are made to rule. We are made to make personal decisions and we will be held accountable.

Gooding says, "I made a choice to be a Christian because I am a free moral agent—no one else is to blame." He chose to believe. Sin and its progressive nature in society seems to have its root in the very soil of universe. But there is a common theme in all the theories about sin and lawlessness. Paul calls it the mystery of iniquity (2 Thessalonians 2:7)! Biblically, there is a common understanding, even a law of the universe.

> Do not be deceived, God is not mocked; for whatever a man sows, that he will also reap. 8 For he who sows to his flesh will of the flesh reap corruption, but he who sows to the Spirit will of the Spirit reap everlasting life. (Galatians 6:7-8)

In early computer language, Garbage in Garbage out—GIGO!

> Then Adoni-Bezek fled, and they pursued him and caught him and cut off his thumbs and big toes. 7 And Adoni-Bezek said, "Seventy kings with their thumbs and big toes cut off used to gather scraps under my table; as I have done, so God has repaid me." (Judges 1:6-7)

What goes around, comes around is the common phrase today.

Paul uses the term, "Flesh." A life turned away from God either willingly or intellectually will reap corruption. A life turned toward God will reap a life of the Spirit.

> Now the works of the flesh are evident, which are: adultery, fornication, uncleanness, lewdness, 20 idolatry, sorcery, hatred, contentions, jealousies, outbursts of wrath, selfish ambitions, dissensions, heresies, 21 envy, murders, drunkenness, revelries, and the like; of which I tell you beforehand, just as I also told you in time past, that those who practice such things will not inherit the kingdom of God. (Galatians 5:19-21)

> But the fruit of the Spirit is love, joy, peace, longsuffering, kindness, goodness, faithfulness, 23 gentleness, self-control. Against such there is no law ... 25 If we live in the Spirit, let us also walk in the Spirit. (Galatians 5:22-23, 25)

God did not ever make you sin, tempt you to sin, or seduce you to sin. And, the demonic, Satan and his principalities and powers are not a match for God.

> Having disarmed principalities and powers, He made a public spectacle of them, triumphing over them in it. (Colossians 2:15)

> For I am persuaded that neither death nor life, nor angels nor principalities nor powers, nor things present nor things to come, 39 nor height nor depth, nor any other created thing, shall be able to separate us from the love of God which is in Christ Jesus our Lord. (Romans 8:38-39)

Joseph lived with setback after setback. Joseph unlearned violence and jealousy. He had to reframe his life in faith. His statements to the very brothers who betrayed him are powerful and show a life framed by the purposes of God.

> Joseph said to his brothers, "Please come near to me." So they came near. Then he said: "I am Joseph your brother, whom you sold into Egypt. 5 But now, do not therefore be grieved or angry with yourselves because you sold me here; for God sent me before you to preserve life. (Genesis 45:4-5)

> "Do not be afraid, for am I in the place of God? 20 But as for you, you meant evil against me; but God meant it for good, in order to bring it about as it is this day, to save many people alive. 21 Now therefore, do not be afraid; I will provide for you and your little ones." And he comforted them and spoke kindly to them. (Genesis 50:19-21)

Joseph successfully reframed his life in faith. It could have been framed in vengeance and anger, but it was not. It could have been framed in bitterness toward God or blame toward his brothers, but it was not. No one is hopeless. You might struggle to believe God loves you because of your rebellion against his calling or your lot in life. You may feel your alcoholism or drug addiction has cost you God's love. You may have had an abortion or abortions, a sordid and foul sexual story, constant breakdowns in relationship, a violent history and feel that God is out to punish you. You may have lived so long in these conditions that you have thrown in the towel. It's just who you are. Really? Is God powerless? Will you cast down the strongholds and cast down the arguments that rise against God in mind. Will you cast off God's design as impossible for you? You can be delivered, and you can walk in dominion.

Think of Job. Job's name means adversary. Indeed, he took an adversarial stance in his prayer to God. It took 42 chapters, but Job finally began to see a world and life he had not seen. It was a spiritual world that he was intimately involved with. Job had a proper theology, but it was not enough to answer or explain the catastrophic events of his life. God is great, certainly. But Job had lived too long on God's great creation and seen injustice, the abusive and violent ways of the wicked in the world's order. He was unrestrained in his complaint that God does not seem to be taking him seriously!

> Job claims that God, "destroys the blameless and the wicked" (Job 9:22).
> And he wished, "Oh, that I had one to hear me! ... That my Prosecutor had written a book! / Surely I would carry it on my shoulder, / And bind it on me like a crown; / I would declare to Him (Job 31:35-37).

In other words, Job first decides to overthrow the divine order of authority, by contending with God, and then decides he will take God to court for not obeying his own laws. Listen, we like theology. But you cannot get your answers to life's calamities from theology or theological surmising. You must know God. You cannot survive on theory! You have to really get saved, and stay saved, if you are going to survive this world and this life.

Job's suffering does not square with his or his friend's conventional explanations and theological clichés. Pastor and Esther Gooding sat in a hospital resident's room with a couple while the doctor came in three times to tell them their baby was very sick. Finally coming in and saying the baby had died. The Doctor then offered to bring them the baby so they could hold her. Angela was cold and blue. I had nothing to say! There wasn't anything to say. There were plenty of tears and sobs. I was there. I felt to some small degree their grief and pain—but theologize, explain, or tell them why? No!

Job waits and waits for God to answer. Then, finally, after a serious confrontation where God does not really answer Job, he replies.

> You [God] asked, 'Who is this that obscures my plans without knowledge?' Surely I spoke of things I did not understand, things too wonderful for me to know. 4 "You said, 'Listen now, and I will speak; I will question you, and you shall answer me.' 5 My ears had heard of you but now my eyes have seen you. 6 Therefore I despise myself and repent in dust and ashes." (Job 42:3-6)

Job had to reframe the calamities of life. He had not framed them in faith. Yes, he dutifully (religiously) maintained his righteous behavior and careful speech. Nonetheless, God understood. Job had spoken and obscured God's plan because he did not frame the events in faith. Job confesses he has learned what he did not know—that is what he had learned in conventional instruction and theology (doctrine) he now knows personally, intimately and in reality. It is not theory.

Culture is the powerful shaper of your life. It comes from many angles because every group of people you are around has a culture. Paul makes a telling statement in Ephesians when he talks about spiritual powers.

> For we do not wrestle against flesh and blood, but against principalities, against powers, against the rulers of the darkness of this age, against spiritual hosts of wickedness in the heavenly places. (Ephesians 6:12)

Every people group has a culture. Clubs have cultures. Extended families have cultures. Gangs have a culture. You can read about the cultures of winning and losing teams. They may be professional teams or College or high school teams but they all have a culture. When you join any group you sign on to be part of a culture. When you go or attend any group you are invited into a culture. Churches have a culture. It's one thing to be delivered but another thing to unlearn the culture of godlessness and become part of the kingdom (culture) of God.

The culture of your family, your friends, your organizations, your job, your school, your ethnic culture, your national culture and many more can powerfully affect how you process and deal with the events of your life. Spiritual warfare is not in the flesh, but against spiritual powers that reign on earth and in heaven.

Our lives are like the layers of an onion. God strips away the old, ugly crusty layer on the outside. That's deliverance. But that is not the last layer of your life. God then peels away a layer at a time. Based largely on decisions as we process life we gain or lose dominion. Most people don't know everything that is inside them until God reveals it through the events of life, through his word and by the Holy Spirit. God peels away the layers to reveal what is more deeply embedded. Our hearts are deceitful. We often do not know all that lies on the inside and all that moves us to do and say what we do and say.

Sin never heals itself. Sin has to be confronted. Everyone has issues that are positive. Everyone also has issues that are negative. Our lives have been likened to a city. John Bunyan wrote the classic story of *Mansoul*. In it, City Hall and the government buildings are filled with workers that labor for the good of the city and its citizens. But there are alleys where there are brothels, bars, pawn shops and illegally run casinos. For the good of the city these things must be brought to the light.

Once, after traveling home from overseas Pastor Campbell, still jet-lagging, played basketball. In the course of the game his old competitive culture of basketball flared and he "slapped the fire" out of one of the players. On another occasion in the foyer of the church he slapped a cigarette out of a young man's mouth. His grandmother was watching. That landed Campbell in court. The judge admonished him saying, "Mr. Campbell, I don't ever want to see your face in here again."

Our problem is we don't always see what is in us for what it is. Issues seem to manifest in believers on Sunday mornings. One Sunday, while stomping around in anger, Campbell knocked over his wife's beautiful antique lamp. His son Brad re-enacted the event for those in church that morning. Pastor Campbell turned around saw his son repeating all the moves in the back of the small church he was pastoring. Campbell could not hear Brad but knew by his actions what was happening. God spoke to Pastor Campbell. "Do you want your whole church to act like that?" It's one thing when the judge corrects you and another when God corrects you.

The issue we must face up to in these areas is that we don't see them as a big deal. We don't see them as something to be confronted. They are flaws that occur in private, or just in the home, or on the athletic field or in some arena that seems insignificant. As long as we are attending church and have a degree of faithfulness these flaws are harnessed and kept in check. In a crisis, however, things are different. In a crisis the devil is trying to take you out. Jesus told Peter the devil wanted to sift him as wheat. There is a demonic strategy to seize the events of life and turn them to the demonic advantage. There are issues and situation crafted for your peculiar weaknesses and flaws.

Dominion is tested and challenged. Pharaoh, a type of the demonic elements of life, did not simply surrender when the Hebrews left Egypt. They left Egypt because the power of God was manifest on that final night of bondage. An angel with the power to kill the firstborn swept through Egypt. The cries of the families who lost their firstborn sons and daughters were heard throughout Egypt. The distinctive truth established that night was that the blood of a lamb over the door caused death to be turned away at the door. But, Pharaoh changed his mind.

Unfaithfulness loses things you once had harnessed and thought were not a big deal. When you quit and leave the church you are away from a restraining power. Outside the body of Christ, surroundings that help and encourage are gone. Backsliding means you will do things you never thought possible and go places you never thought you would. Backsliding is a life once delivered but not lived in dominion. Deliverance is what God does. Dominion is something you must incorporate in your life by decisions and choices.

Dominion occurs when you surrender to God's will. Whenever you surrender to God you become powerful. When you resist or refuse to surrender to God then you are vulnerable to a demonic takeover of your life. Five times in Exodus Moses says "let my people go" for worship and service to God. Following the night of the Death Angel's sweep Pharaoh "called for Moses and Aaron by night, and said, "Rise, go out from among my people, both you and the children of Israel. And go, serve the Lord as you have said (Exodus 12:31)."

Dave Marks asked the homeless people and others about their story. There is one they tell themselves. There is one they use to explain the conditions of their life. The problem is their story does not account for a way to move ahead.

This scripture says our weapons are *mighty* in God. And it says they are for pulling down, casting down and demolishing the arguments and strategies of hell. They are for taking dominion in life. These weapons enable one to cast down all that opposes God. That is dominion.

You can have dominion in one area, but not in others. Where you do not have dominion you will have trouble. Unconquered dimensions of life will be problems until dominion is gained.

Life happens to us all. It is in many ways unpredictable except for the fact that it is unpredictable. The economy changes. The weather changes. The seasons change. The day to day events that seem so predictable often change. They can change abruptly and without warning. People suffer in accidents and changes in health. Relationships among siblings, in married couples, between friends and business partners can change. Often change is unexpected, unwanted or surprising. We can be blindsided by events in life. We do not have to be defeated.

Dominion is found wherever Jesus is Lord. Wherever Jesus is allowed to rule is where you'll find dominion.

CHAPTER 3

DO YOU HAVE DOMINION?

Why do I do the things I do?

It is a good question to ask, "Do I have dominion?" Or, "do circumstances, other people and my own emotions bounce me around? Do I live a life filled with purpose and control or am I just moved along by factors out of my control?"

There is a common phenomenon among young people. It is common enough to get a name. It's called the "Turkey Drop." It refers to teens who are paired off as sweethearts. They go through high school as sweethearts. Then, they go to college or join the military and are separated. Sometimes one goes away and the other stays home. When they are home for Thanksgiving, they are sweethearts and together again. When they leave after "Turkey Day" they are no longer sweethearts. It's the Turkey Drop. Somehow absence has not made the heart grow fonder. One victim of a Turkey Drop was so disturbed he went to his counselor. They talked about the struggle to maintain a long-distance relationship. Finally, the counselor asked him, "How good a relationship did you have?"[1] It's a good question to ask when talking about dominion.

Dominion depends on a faith relationship with Jesus. If you live your life in Jesus and the word of God, your life will be different. It will be different from those who live for the cares of the world. Your life will be different than when you were unsaved and unredeemed. It will be different than when you lived in rebellion and resistance to God. It will be a life of dominion.

Your life can have dominion when you neighbor's life is crashing. You can have dominion in your marriage when the marriage in the apartment next door is in chaos. Your finances can be in order and working for you while those of your relatives are in constant turmoil. Your relationships can have peace when those around you are filled with violence, strife and anger. Sometimes the question, "Do you have dominion?" must be answered in terms of "How good is your relationship with Jesus?"

God saves and delivers. But salvation is not just an event. It is not just something we do before moving on to other "bucket list" experiences. Being saved is not a religious phase. It is life. Deliverance, however, does not guarantee a life of dominion. The miracle of salvation is a work of Christ accomplished on Calvary. That is deliverance, but that is not all there is to salvation. You can never be more saved than at the moment you surrender your life to Jesus. Just as you can never be "more" human than you were at birth. But there is more to life than birth and more to salvation than the event. Israel was delivered. Once they passed through the Red Sea they were free. Pharaoh, Pharaoh's chariots and Pharaoh's army were destroyed. Israel, however, was not yet to their destiny. They were not yet to the Promised Land. There was still a walk to be made in their newfound freedom. There was a destiny to be possessed. There was a transforming life of dominion to be gained. The old slave mentalities had to be transformed. The institutionalized lifestyle and mindset had to be transformed before they entered the Promised Land. In one of the world's greatest tragedies an entire generation, save two persons, failed in their freedom.

Traveling to Israel—and many other places, especially in the Near East—one sees what appear to be large hills. They seem to be out of place. They do not appear to be part of the natural geology. These are an archeologist's delight. They are sites of ancient cities that have been destroyed time and again. Each conquering people has built their own city on top of the ruins of the previous city. In Israel, excavations have exposed layer upon layer of building. These mounds or hills are called "tells." Pastor Wayman Mitchell, the leader of a fellowship of 2500 churches, commented one day in Israel, "Life is a tell." It is a story. Indeed, a life does "tell" a story. Archeology is the art and science of uncovering these various layers and piecing together the history of the cities and their people.

Our lives are just that way. They are built layer on layer, one atop the other. Each event, good or bad, rest atop the previous layers of events, activities and happenings. Each sin, self-willed act, disaster, set-back, calamity, abuse or circumstance has made an impact. We have become what we are through these many events. Every one is shaped and molded by the cultural mores and behaviors of our lives.

This is often explained like peeling an onion. Once the outer layers are off, there remains layer upon layer of onion. Our salvation can be viewed that way. Once we are saved and "cleaned up" a little. Many people assume that is all there is. But as we continue, we discover there are a lot of things in us that are still not the way they are supposed to be. They are not yet transformed. Many of our old reactions and attitudes are still with us. God has brought us out of sin by his mighty power. Nonetheless a lot of work remains to be done.

Someone has commented that it was easier to get the children of Israel out of Egypt than it was to get Egypt out of them. We approach life so we are not hurt. We grow up and live in a cultural system. We know the rules—that is, how the system worked. And we know many systems that affect our lives. We could have become part of the welfare system. We may have been affected and learned the penal system, the gang system, the racial system or some other cultural system. We are systematically shaped by "The System" in whatever culture(s) we have been in.

Israel lived in slavery. It was a system. Biblically, we have all been slaves to sin. Slavery is a culture. Tens of thousands of slaves following the Civil War in the United States were suddenly freed by the Emancipation Proclamation. Like Israel coming out of Egypt, it happened overnight. One day they were slaves and the next they were free. The shocking reality, however, was that many—maybe most—never left the plantation.

The popular social advocate and media commentator, Star Parker, told about her grandfather's experience. Her grandfather determined to do something with his emancipation. He determined to peel off the layer of slavery from his life. He made a decision that the cultural mold of slavery was going to be peeled away. His edict was, "Buy property and a gun." He was one generation away from slavery. He made a choice in 1905. He was free. He determined to live it. He did. He bought land and a gun. He was able to buy and keep enough land to set up his children and grandchildren in their own homes before he passed away. Today all of them could retire on property in Traveler's Rest, South Carolina. Star Parker's portion was two-and-a-half acres.[2] Most of those emancipated, like Israel, did not possess their freedom to become all that was possible. Many went back to the plantation and, like Israel, did not experience the Promised Land.

You can live with the mindsets and cultural norms of your past. It is possible to remain in the old slave culture where everything was met with murmuring, complaining, bickering and assuming that everyone who had anything was out to get yours. It is what Israel did. They met every obstacle they faced in the wilderness with murmuring and complaining against leadership. Rather than pray for all who are in authority over them, the old mind set was to curse those who had rule over them.

In a slave community, whether in Israel or some other place, children are not your own—they could be bought and sold. In the slave mindset a lover could be used by someone else, sold or simply taken away. To build a home, a marriage or raise children was not guaranteed. It was instead, unlikely. Everything could change overnight and often did. The reality of that tenuous existence triggered mindsets of holding everything at arms-length. They feared getting married or committed to love and attachment. It was a life of "use or be used." It is possible to live that way, but it is not dominion. It will not bring you into the Promised Land.

Hundreds of thousands of God's children were delivered by the mighty hand of God but perished in the wilderness because they still acted and thought as slaves. They had obtained their freedom. They were still enslaved in their minds. They were insecure and distrustful of their leadership. On more than one occasion they accused Moses and Aaron—and God—of bringing them out into the wilderness to kill them. They expected everything to be provided like they expected straw to be provided when they were making bricks in Egypt. They perished because they did not know how to frame their lives. They perished because they put God to the test to "see" if he was really among them (Exodus 17:7, Deuteronomy 6:16). They did not frame their life in faith.

The Book of Hebrews contains faith's "Hall of Fame." Chapter eleven deals with faith. It says, "By faith we understand ... that the things which are seen were not made of things which are visible." The Hebrews did not see themselves as conquerors. They did not see themselves as delivered. They did not grasp freedom. Their frame of reference was slavery. They processed events as they had in Egypt. Always in their mind was the fear of being hurt, abandoned, abused, or even killed. They rejoiced at crossing the sea but plunged into depression at the first bitter experience. The bitter waters of Marah tested them. At the bitter point in life they could not see that God was among them.

David McCullough is one of America's greatest historians. His books include, *1776, Truman, John Adams,* and *The Great Bridge.* A collection of commencement addresses he has delivered to colleges over the last several years is in *The American Spirit: Who We Are and What We Stand For.* In it he highlights significant contributors to the American story. The address to Dartmouth College in 1999 is titled "What's Essential is Invisible." He takes the line from the classic fable, *The Little Prince,* first published in 1943. It is a fable about the world of imagination versus the world seen naturally. McCullough uses the line in reference to presidential power.

Power has to do with so many intangibles for which there is no real "measurement." Authority cannot be measured by any empirical means, but it is real. Power, he says, is the integrity of George Washington, the soul of Abraham Lincoln, the courage of Harry Truman, the charm of John Kennedy and the clarity of a Ronald Reagan press conference. What is essential—what is truly important—he writes, is invisible.[3]

What's important, the writer of Hebrews says, is not merely what can be seen. God established the world by his word. His word is eternal. His word is essential. His word is important. Yet, it is unseen. The creation is one of the most commonly missed revelations God gives us about his eternal power and godhead. It is framed by God's word. Dominion is a quality of life that is vital yet unseen. "Framed" means God established creation for a purpose. Creation is structured for a function. It is made the way it is for God's purpose.

The word "framed" has different connotations or meanings for different people. An artist and a carpenter probably view the word "framed" differently. For the artist the frame separates the art from the rest of the world. The frame sets off the beauty of the artwork against the commonness of the wall it hangs on. For the carpenter and builder, the frame is what everything hangs on. It is what supports the structure and makes it useful. It is what supports the structure of the building making it useful. The world is framed so that God can dwell among us, with us, and in us. Dominion depends on how you frame your life in God's kingdom.

Star Parker's birth name was LarStella—a contraction of her two aunt's names, Stella and Laura. She explained it was a residual from the slave era when children could be sold and never found again. Blacks in the South commonly mixed names of relatives just in case. Her mindset was, "Life is chance, and values are relative. I can do whatever I think is right." It was what she learned on her stereo, on her television and in the public schools. She learned it was a white man's world designed to keep her from getting ahead. She was convinced it was a racist world where, "If [she] didn't get them, they would get [her]."

When she was confronted by a pastor saying that God was to be her "source" and not the government she reacted against the thought.

Mainstream life was totally foreign to her. Didn't this pastor know it was a white man's world? Didn't he know it was about luck in a dog-eat-dog world? This pastor, Ken, looked her in the eye and said her "lifestyle was unacceptable to God." She was twenty-six years old. It was easy to reject the concept of faith. In her mind all absolutes were judgmental. That is, they were excessive criticism of people. She made a decision to peel away a layer of institutionalized living. "Stepping out," she said, "would require a deep-rooted trust to turn my finite well-being over to the caring hands of an infinite God." She made a decision to learn how to live free.[4]

Some of the layers of life that often need to be peeled away are attitudes about God, about life, about people, about relationships, about the future, and about what you will become. Some things that need to be peeled away are visible and well known to others. Reactions to criticism, outbursts of anger and body language are visible and seen by all. Other things are unseen such as how you talk to yourself, the things you fear and the heartaches that still affect your faith. These things, visible and invisible, affect how we handle the events of life. Deliverance from Egypt brought Israel into a land and circumstances that were unfamiliar and challenging. Dominion is a spiritual dimension and quality of life that is primarily inside. It essential, though often invisible.

It has been commonly noted in various forms and ways that "Life Happens." In other words, we do not control everything. Jim Fixx, author of *The Complete Book of Running,* said that when he ran, "I feel like I am in control of my body." Even so, at age 52, after his morning run in Vermont he died of a fulminate (explosive or rapidly escalating) heart attack. We are never in as much control as we might think. What you see is not all there is. Likewise, what you feel is not all there is.

We live making decisions based on what we see and what we feel. God asks us to live by faith. Often, we think if we had better circumstances—what we see—we would be better able to control our destinies. Happiness and dominion are seen to be products of circumstances. We often believe it is our circumstances that hinder us. When we allow circumstances to dictate our feelings and decisions we lose dominion.

Professor Laurie Santos of Yale University noted the general unhappiness of students at the university and set out to help. She created the class *Psychology 157: Psychology and the Good Life*. It became the most popular class in Yale's history and one of the most talked about courses in America. She says, "College students are much more overwhelmed, much more stressed, much more anxious, and much more depressed than they have ever been. I think we really have a crisis writ large at colleges in how students are doing in terms of self-care and mental health," adding, "Sadly, I don't think it's just in colleges." College students are not alone in feeling helpless and hopeless. Many experience this lack of dominion.

The idea for the class was triggered when professor Santos saw data from the American College Health Association's findings about student depression. They found fifty-two-percent of students report feeling hopeless and thirty-nine-percent suffered from depression. Student depression was so severe, some found it difficult to function during the previous year. Literally, they had no dominion over the affairs of student life or their emotions.

Twelve hundred Yale students signed up for her class. The prerequisite for the class was to take the "Authentic Happiness Inventory" offered online by the University of Pennsylvania. Another way to do the inventory is to make a short list of the things you think would make you happier. The first day of class you find out none of the things you listed would really make you happier.

> "Nearly everything you think will make you happier won't, because nearly everything you're likely to list—assuming of course that your basic life needs are taken care of—is some circumstantial change: more money, a different home or job, a long vacation, or even that enticing snack that lies just beyond the vending machine's glass."

Current research from the University of California, Riverside notes that happiness is about 50 percent determined by genetics. Some babies we call happy babies, and some are called colicky babies. Roughly forty-percent is determined by how you process life—attitudes, thoughts and actions. Only ten-percent is determined by your circumstances. The takeaway is we assume that circumstances are the biggest factor in happiness. We overestimate how important circumstances are. And we grossly underestimate how important changing our behavior affects our sense of well-being. What we believe would make the biggest difference in our happiness, doesn't. We often overlook the true sources of happiness and well-being. Happy people are consistently shown to be people who devote time to family and friends, practice gratitude, are optimistic, and physically active enjoying the present. The first lesson of the class is that happiness is something worth working at.[5]

Biblically, this is easily seen to be the case for happiness and dominion. Circumstances are not the largest determinants of happiness, well-being, or dominion. A guest lecturer said,

> "A lot of people of think happiness as a very, very exciting emotion. They expect it to be this constant state of ecstasy—as opposed to a sustainable and attainable form of happiness, almost like quiet joy. It doesn't look like winning the lottery. It looks much more like your life is actually wonderful."[6]

Happiness, however defined, is not exactly dominion. Dominion is not determined by circumstances. Dominion doesn't look like a Senior Drill Instructor dressing down a squad of new recruits. And it doesn't feel like winning the lottery. It doesn't look like someone who never sees difficulties or setbacks in life. It is possible to make a case, King David had more dominion while hiding in a cave with four hundred distressed, debt ridden, and discontent men (1 Samuel 22:1), than Saul sitting in the palaces of government with the wealth and army of the nation in his power.

Dominion is a spiritual issue. It is a spiritual dimension beyond circumstances. Think about the issues of Paul's life. He lists some of them in 2nd Corinthians.

> For we do not want you to be ignorant, brethren, of our trouble which came to us in Asia: that we were burdened beyond measure, above strength, so that we despaired even of life. 9 Yes, we had the sentence of death in ourselves, that we should not trust in ourselves but in God who raises the dead, 10 who delivered us from so great a death, and does deliver us; in whom we trust that He will still deliver us, 11 you also helping together in prayer for us, that thanks may be given by many persons on our behalf for the gift granted to us through many. (2 Corinthians 1:8-11)

And in chapter 4, he again presents a list.

> We are hard-pressed on every side, yet not crushed; we are perplexed, but not in despair; 9 persecuted, but not forsaken; struck down, but not destroyed— 10 always carrying about in the body the dying of the Lord Jesus, that the life of Jesus also may be manifested in our body. 11 For we who live are always delivered to death for Jesus' sake, that the life of Jesus also may be manifested in our mortal flesh. 12 So then death is working in us, but life in you. 13 And since we have the same spirit of faith, according to what is written, "I believed and therefore I spoke," we also believe and therefore speak, 14 knowing that He who raised up the Lord Jesus will also raise us up with Jesus, and will present us with you. (2 Corinthians 4:8-14)

Paul's reaction to all these events is not what one might expect.

> Therefore we do not lose heart. Even though our outward man is perishing, yet the inward man is being renewed day by day. 17 For our light affliction, which is but for a moment, is working for us a far more exceeding and eternal weight of glory, 18 while we do not look at the things which are seen, but at the things which are not seen. For the things which are seen are temporary, but the things which are not seen are eternal. (2 Corinthians 4:16-18)

What you see is *not* all there is. The setbacks, dilemmas and obstacles in Paul's life are powerful and experienced by everyone. They are so familiar to some that they can read them and not even see them as part of Paul's life. He says he is troubled more than is bearable. He despairs of life itself. In chapter four he says he is hard-pressed from all sides, perplexed (baffled, not understanding what is going on), persecuted, struck-down (physically and in sickness), constantly dying to self, at death's door, and with death working in his being. That is not all he says, however. He also says, "We believe." Paul is not talking about his life as a sinner. He is talking about the life he lives following deliverance from the old life. He is living in dominion. His "therefore" acknowledges his personal salvation and deliverance and because of that he, "does not lose heart." How is that? He does not limit his vision to the things that are seen. Those things are passing away.

Many struggle with dominion because they connect their circumstances to their sense of well-being without a connection to their deliverance and faith. When the focus is on the things that are seen, dominion is lost. The loss of dominion over situations and circumstances is commonly played out by people who see themselves as a victim or by blaming others for their circumstances. Jesus came to a man at the Pool of Bethesda and asked if he wanted to be well. The man answered, "Sir, I have no man to put me into the pool when the water is stirred up; but while I am coming, another steps down before me (John 5:7)." These are common answers for a person's circumstances. They formulate a plausible excuse for why they have been afflicted thirty-eight years. Or, they blame others. People lacking dominion use the excuse of no one to help them or always someone else gets there first.

If we think about Jesus, we can understand a bit more. Jesus had no place to lay his head. He suffered rejection more than any other man. He experienced the rejection of his Father, neighbors and family. He was accused of being a drunkard, a false prophet and his own village thought him worthy of death. He was accused of being a liar and not sent by God. He appeared to be powerless to heal himself or come down from the cross. Nathaniel said to Philip, "Can any good thing come out of Nazareth? (John 1:6)." The prophet Isaiah says of the him:

> He is despised and rejected by men, A Man of sorrows and acquainted with grief. And we hid, as it were, our faces from Him; He was despised, and we did not esteem Him. (Isaiah 53:3)

It is certainly true that circumstances can be bad. It can even be they can go from bad to worse. What you see and what you feel, however, do not produce dominion. Dominion is fostered by faith. Dominion frames the events of life—good and bad—in faith. The word of God becomes the reality to live by. Dominion, far more than happiness, is worth working at. Paul's comment is "We do not lose heart." This is a choice Paul and his companions made. Then Paul adds because the "inward man is being renewed day by day." Is it you? Is it happening in you? When what you see is not working, when your world is crashing down around you or wave after surging wave of turmoil smashes into you, do you have dominion? Do you, as Paul says, "Believe and therefore speak?" What you say to yourself and others is important to your dominion.

Being a victim of circumstances is not the only mindset hindering dominion. We often mistake wealth for dominion. Indeed, this was the mindset of the Hebrew culture in Jesus day and remains so for many people today. Wealth was assumed to be the measure of a person's spirituality. People believe it today of themselves and others. If they are blessed, they assume they must be alright with God. If you follow the headlines of the wealthy you know they are as likely as any other person to blow-up their marriage, cave in to corruption or have outbursts of insanity in their lives. People think if they had wealth, they would have dominion. If I had wealth, the thinking goes, I could obtain what I need. If I had wealth, I could be someone. Some people believe, if they had wealth, they would have respect. Of course, many people believe that wealth would buy happiness.

In the same Yale class, a guest speaker, Michael Norton of the Harvard Business School, said, "The biggest misconception is that more will be better. We did a survey of millionaires and asked, 'How much more money would you need ....' Those with $1 million said, 'three times as much.' But people with $3 million also said, 'Three times as much.' So it went, all the way up." So, if you have, say, $30 million, you would need $90 million! Or, if you had $90 million it would take $270 million to make you happy! It seems that at some point you would just have to be unhappy!

The reality is that Jesus had dominion over the demonic and did not have large money. Not only did Jesus have no place to lay his head he sent Peter to get a coin out of a fish's mouth to pay his temple tax. Recently a young man was arrested for murder. He answered a listing for a used X-box. He made the arrangements and met the kid selling it. He killed him and took the X-box. He was caught, arrested and is facing charges of murder and theft. Several years ago, a young man killed another for his *Air Jordan* tennis shoes believing he would be someone if he had those shoes. Wealth and possessions do not establish dominion.

In much of the world it is felt that getting ahead is about your connections. Access through the back door is possible because you have a connection. This is common in the world. "It's not who you are, it is who you know," is the familiar statement. It's true that sometimes things are easier if you have favor with someone who can help you. But knowing connected people is not the same as dominion.

A new convert in the church came to the pastor and said he was famous. He could walk into any club and people knew him. The pastor explained to him there were better places to be known. He changed his view of fame and connections and is pastoring today. A few years ago the classic "anchor-person" on the local Phoenix news station was at a party and became unruly. When the police were escorting her away she was heard screaming, "Do you know who I am? Do you know who I am." In other words, "I am a person with pull." She thought her connections were the key to dominion. She lost her job and became a nobody again. Connections were not the same as dominion.

Position, social status, money, race, and many other things people seek do not produce dominion. Recently an Arizona legislator was stopped for erratic driving. He was arrested for driving under the influence of alcohol. Having not learned the lesson of the news anchor, he said, "I hope you know who you are arresting." It didn't seem to give him any dominion with the arresting officer. He said, "It's Ok, my wife works for the Department of Motor Vehicles," implying that she would "fix" things for him. He only succeeded in becoming the topic of a morning full of jokes on the local radio stations. Without dominion you'll act and say crazy things. Things that will hurt you. Things and words that will not help you. You'll never gain dominion by bullying or acting on just what you see and feel. What you see is *not* all there is.

There are many mindsets that are not centered on faith. They are issues of the heart that must be surrendered to God. Following their deliverance, Israel entered the wilderness. The Israelites were unfamiliar with the wilderness because for generations they had lived in bondage to Pharaoh. They had never traveled anywhere apart from Pharaoh's building projects, with only a dirt floor to sleep on, under a limited shelter. In the wilderness God was preparing them for his presence "with them."

Dominion is a spiritual dimension resident in you. "For we walk by faith, not by sight (2 Corinthians 5:7)." Dominion means you *rule* in your own life. Dominion is how you deal with the uncertainties in life. Dominion is how you deal with the wildernesses and the barren places of your life. Dominion is about how you deal with the events and occasions that cause perplexity. Dominion is needed when there are multiple opinions and options. Dominion keeps one on course through the narrow and difficult places that everyone experiences. Dominion is about control over reactions Someone has said, "It is easier to act like a Christian than it is to react like a Christian." And reactions depend on how we think. Joseph Sittler, the late professor at Chicago University has commented concerning David's Psalm, "Yea, though I walk through the valley of the shadow of death, I will fear no evil (Psalm 23:4)." He noted that we walk through the valley of death just once, we spend our entire life in the shadow.

Dominion is about real life. It is not a fiction. It is not a worked-up emotion. Dominion must be real when you are dry or feeling burned out on the mundane every day job, and begin to look around. People suffer boredom. The novelist Walker Percy calls it, "The self being stuffed with itself." That is something like saying, you are bored because you are boring. We look to the other side of the fence for a better or newer place to be bored. When the marriage is stressed or strained by finances, children, disagreements and false relatives, then other people begin to look attractive and pleasant to be around. When we lack dominion, we are vulnerable to demonic seduction and distraction. Difficult circumstances and alternative scenarios begin to play on the mind. Suddenly, it seems, an easier way appears.

The old nature begins to exercise itself. The old culture and old lifestyle are not remembered as bad. The Hebrews began to fantasize about Egypt and their life there. Sometimes people begin to think of the old "high" or the so-called "first time." One can remember the fun of getting drunk and forget the bad that followed. One man told me when he was too drunk to know what he was doing, "But I like it (beer)." Sometimes events can be glorified out of proportion.

> Once in saintly passion,
> I cried, with desperate grief,
> "O Lord, my heart is black with guilt; Of sinners I am chief."
> Then stooped my guardian angel,
> And whispered from behind,
> "Vanity, my little man; You're nothing of the kind."[7]

Paul was a game changer. Paul was a world changer. He had dominion. He didn't change the world because he was the man with the best 'abs' in the gym. He didn't change the world because he was full of the world's wisdom. No, Paul was accused of being a weakling. He was a man without the perfect body or speech. When Paul boasted he boasted about his weakness. He did not boast about his successes, power, or exploits but rather about his vulnerability and weakness. Paul is not the model of the modern wanna-be world changer. Some are trying to keep a sharp image by lying on their *Facebook* page. People strive for large followings on Twitter and other social media. Paul exposed his weaknesses. Paul was real.

Dominion means there is a resident quality within that is not driven by image or personal agenda. A person with dominion is not spinning events and circumstances so they personally look good. Paul says he came to Corinth after having a difficult time in Philippi. He was imprisoned in Philippi despite having great spiritual success. In Thessalonica he had fierce opposition and had to leave in the night. In Berea, after seemingly initial success, the crowds were stirred up by unbelieving Jews. The brethren took Paul to the sea and then by boat to Athens. In Athens, Paul spoke to the philosophers. Not much occurred in terms of church planting and discipleship. So, Paul says he came to Corinth "knowing only Jesus Christ and him crucified (1 Corinthians 2:1-5)." In Corinth there was a demonstration of the power and Spirit of God. He came in weakness. He did not come boasting about his wisdom or excellent speaking. He had dominion.

Throughout his ministry Paul had dominion. He did not lose heart or abandon the mission. Paul said he had not been "disobedient to the heavenly vision (Acts 26:19)," at his hearing before Festus the Governor, and King Agrippa.

Without dominion people are stressed, uptight about events and driven throughout the day. They leave no time for God. They are like the doubtful person James describes. "He who doubts is like a wave of the sea driven and tossed by the wind (James 1:6)." Dominion is a choice to take responsibility for one's personal behavior and thought life. Paul says, "When I was a child, I spoke as a child, I understood as a child, I thought as a child; but when I became a man, I put away childish things (1 Corinthians 13:11)."

If we ponder that statement, we can understand that maturity—putting away childish things—was a decision Paul made by faith. Paul sees, he says, "in a mirror, dimly," and knows only "in part." By faith he says, "I shall know just as I also am known." Paul is living life in the uncertainty of circumstances we all live in. Paul, and the Hebrews in the wilderness, did not have a blueprint or roadmap. By faith they understood there was a promise of a heavenly and eternal destiny. To order their affairs they had to make decisions seeing and knowing only in part. This is only possible when life is bounded by faith and the word of God.

By faith Paul knew certain things were necessary. Paul knew that his flesh and his thought life had to be brought under subjection to what God had framed for his life. He says, "Therefore I run thus: not with uncertainty. Thus I fight: not as one who beats the air (1 Corinthians 9:26)." The uncertainty for Paul was not God—it was Paul. Moses faced uncertainty about Moses, not God. The children of Israel floundered in their uncertainty about God, not themselves.

To have dominion means you are not soon shaken by events and circumstances even when they seem negative. If we are steady and not soon shaken or distracted, God always has a way of turning events. Paul's salutation to his brethren in ministry encourages faith. "Therefore, my beloved brethren, be steadfast, immovable, always abounding in the work of the Lord, knowing that your labor is not in vain in the Lord (1 Corinthians 15:58)."

Dominion is manifest in the storm. Jesus had dominion. He was not intimidated by the storms. In the physical storm he was asleep and had to be awakened by the fearful disciples. "Teacher," they said, "Do You not care that we are perishing (Mark 4:38)?" Dominion is highlighted in the storms and battles of life. Jesus did not fear what the disciples feared.

Is God involved? Does God care? Of course, God is involved in your life. Of course, God cares. But without dominion we become pensive about the future. Our mood changes when circumstances change and become uncertain. We begin thinking of what might happen. Our imagination can run wild with scenarios and of what could happen. There is no peace when dominion is lacking. People often say, "Pastor, you just don't know what I am going through." The disciples were convinced that Jesus—who had dominion—was unconcerned and didn't know about the events and storm surrounding them. It is often the case that people with dominion are viewed uncaring. People wonder why they do not seem to be responding in fear or mood swings and unthinking language.

People lacking dominion measure others by emotions. Dominion means having a word from God. Abigail seeing that David was ready to kill her husband Nabal and their household rushed to intercept him. She had a word from God that changed everything. David told her, "Go up in peace to your house (2 Samuel 25:32-35)."

A word from God changes everything. A word from God calmed the storm. A word from God was a game changer for David and Abigail. A word from God will calm the storm in your life.

When Paul was on his way to Rome as a prisoner, the ship encountered a horrific storm. Although warned beforehand by Paul, the ship's owner insisted on setting sail. The tempest caught the ship and for many days they were driven up and down the Adriatic Sea. Finally, Paul stood in the midst of them and implored the sailors to be encouraged. He had a word from God.

> Men, you should have listened to me, and not have sailed from Crete and incurred this disaster and loss. 22 And now I urge you to take heart, for there will be no loss of life among you, but only of the ship. 23 For there stood by me this night an angel of the God to whom I belong and whom I serve, 24 saying, 'Do not be afraid, Paul; you must be brought before Caesar; and indeed God has granted you all those who sail with you.' 25 Therefore take heart, men, for I believe God that it will be just as it was told me." (Acts 27:21-25)

As they neared land Paul again implored the souls on board to take sustenance and repeated the promise that no lives would be lost.

A word from God makes a difference. It is the difference between dominion and acting like the old self you used to be. The prophets had a word from God for the nation. Elijah had a word for Ahab (1 Kings 21) and a word for his son Ahaziah (2 Kings 1). Had they heeded the word from God their world would not have collapsed all around them. Nathan had a word from God for David that changed his world (2 Samuel 12). Elisha had a word for the widow, the Shunammite woman (2 Kings 4) and the leper Naaman (2 Kings 5). They were words that changed everything about their lives. These were words of deliverance, health and dominion. They were words they could build their lives and futures around.

Elisabeth Elliot whose husband was famously murdered by the Auca Indians of South America said, "Refuse self-pity. Refuse it absolutely. It is a deadly thing with power to destroy you. Turn your thoughts to Christ who has already carried your griefs and sorrows." Self-pity she says has a power to twist your mind and destroy you. The famous missionary to India, E. Stanley Jones says, "You can rescue out of every unjust, impossible situation something that makes that situation not confining but contributing." Trouble comes to everyone. A word from God can secure your future and deliver from the demonic strategy to twist your mind and destroy your life.

God's word cuts to healing and deliverance. It separates the divine from the worldly, the sacred from the common and orders the mind in truth. God's word severs from the old life. The words of God mend and bind up the wounds for the new life of Christ. Have you ever asked yourself, "Do I have a word from God?" Are you just driven pillar to post by the circumstances of your life? Have you ever stopped and asked yourself, "Why do I behave like I do?"

Dominion does not just fall out of the sky. When you are driven by the winds of life you have no time for God. Are you always running around trying to mend your image, fix your agenda or reaching for the intangible something that will satisfy the cravings of life? God's desire is to dwell with you and in you. God will not live where you resist or refuse him. When there is no submission to the will of God then God does not dwell there.

Dominion is found in the presence of Jesus. It is found when you live in his presence and when Jesus lives in you. Whatever you surrender to Jesus becomes a source of dominion. Whatever you surrender to the will of God becomes a place of power in your life. God brought the Hebrews out of bondage. They were emancipated. They were set free. Emancipation does not mean walking off the plantation in freedom and then doing your own thing on the streets.

Think about God's purpose. Why would God reach down into the chaos and deplorable conditions of the slave world to deliver the Hebrew children? Yes, they were God's children. Yes, they were living in deplorable conditions. Yes, there was a need in their lives. But there were many widows and many lepers, many blind and many people with desperate needs in other places. God says:

> I will dwell among the children of Israel and will be their God. 46 And they shall know that I am the Lord their God, who brought them up out of the land of Egypt, that I may dwell among them. I am the Lord their God. (Exodus 29:45-46)

> For you are the temple of the living God. As God has said: "I will dwell in them And walk among them. I will be their God, And they shall be My people." (2 Corinthians 6:16-17)

At Christmas we hear and sing, *Emmanuel*. "Emmanuel, Emmanuel, He's God with us." That is what Emmanuel means—God with us. In the Old Testament they carried the tabernacle wherever they traveled. It was God with us. That was his tent. Today our bodies are the tent God dwells in. What was at one time a mystery is now made clear in the work of Jesus.

> The mystery which has been hidden from ages and from generations, but now has been revealed to His saints. 27 To them God willed to make known what are the riches of the glory of this mystery among the Gentiles: which is Christ in you, the hope of glory. (Colossians 1:26-27)

There is dominion wherever Christ reigns. Dominion is not a mystery. It is when you want and allow God to rule in your life. When Christ reigns in your heart your world changes. And it stays changed when you stay in Christ and Christ in you. The scripture admonishes, "If indeed you continue in the faith, grounded and steadfast, and are not moved away from the hope of the gospel which you heard (Colossians 1:23)." It means something to be a child of God. It is more than just deliverance. Hebrews 8:10 says, "For this is the covenant that I will make with the house of Israel after those days, says the Lord: I will put My laws in their mind and write them on their hearts; and I will be their God, and they shall be My people."

Paul notes the issue concerning his own life when he writes in Philippians, "But what things were gain to me, these I have counted loss for Christ. Yet indeed I also count all things loss for the excellence of the knowledge of Christ Jesus my Lord, for whom I have suffered the loss of all things, and count them as rubbish, that I may gain Christ." Modern preaching is generally soft on personal responsibility. Not many are willing to look the Star Parker's of the world in the eye and say, "Your lifestyle is unacceptable to God." Hence, not many make the move by faith to take responsibility for their own life and behavior. Not everything will be done for you. Don't miss the fact that Israel was delivered, yet still had to walk to the promised land. We have a walk to walk. We must walk worthy of Christ. Dominion is about living in Jesus and Jesus living in you.

Joseph C. Campbell and John W. Gooding

CHAPTER 4

"THE 35": DECISIONS MAKE FOR DESTINY

Now it came to pass (Ruth 1:1)

In 1947 Danny Kahneman and his parents arrived in Israel from Europe. They were Jewish immigrants. They survived WWII by hiding in southern France where they lived for a time in chicken coops. They rented an apartment in Jerusalem. Danny quickly learned Hebrew. At home he and his mother spoke French often in angry terms. His sister left home as quickly as she could. It was not a happy home (Lewis, 65). On May 14, 1948 Israel declared independence and the British soldiers left. The armies of Jordan, Syria and Egypt attacked Israel. The Kahneman apartment was close to the new border of the Palestinian State. One day a bullet passed through Danny's bedroom. On another day his scout leader was killed by a bullet. He said life didn't feel particularly dangerous. In France he had been the hunted during WWII. Now, "It was so completely different. Because you are fighting. That is why it is better. I *hated* the status of being a Jew in Europe. I didn't want to be hunted. I didn't want to be a rabbit (Lewis, 61)."

One night in January 1948 Arab fighters had blockaded a group of Jewish settlers in the south. Thirty-eight Jewish soldiers left the basement of Danny's apartment to rescue them. One hurt his ankle and he with two helpers turned back. The rest intended to march through the night and arrive at the settlement before dawn. At dawn they were still on their way. They met an Arab shepherd and marched on. The shepherd informed the Arabs who ambushed them. All thirty-five were killed (Lewis, 62). The group became known simply as "The 35."

They were killed because they could not bring themselves to shoot a shepherd. The decision took only a moment and was based on intuition, emotion, subjective memories and comparisons with other shepherds. The decision cost them their lives. How you process events is one of the critical factors of making decisions. Far too often decisions are made on the basis of a feeling or a hunch. Decisions, however, lead to destiny.

Following the war Danny Kahneman was allowed to choose a path in the Hebrew University. He applied for the psychology department. The department head was killed in an ambush and the dream of a psychology department at the university died with him. Danny would spend his life studying decisions. Freud was "popular" at that time. "Danny didn't want anyone lying on his couch, and he didn't want to lie on anyone else's. He'd decided to attach no particular importance to his own childhood experience, or even his memories (Lewis, 68)." The events of his past would not be the defining elements of his life.

One of the university instructors loved to tell the story of a donkey placed in the center of a room with two piles of hay equally distant. The moral of the story as it is often told was the donkey starved to death because of indecision. The instructor, who must have had some farm experience, said no country donkey would do that. Only the donkeys you read about in the newspaper would die of indecision. The country donkey would wander over and eat from one pile and then wander over to the other pile and graze there for a while. The point he was making was that it is only when *people* make decisions that things get complicated. And when donkeys make decisions people are supposed to make you can read about those in the papers every day (Lewis, 68).

Danny's quest was to answer the question behavioral psychologists should answer but ignore. How does the brain create meaning? Why do people with the same tools and capacity experience different outcomes? That was the question put to the Israeli Defense Forces by top US generals. How is it people with the same tools (weapons—rifles, tanks and airplanes) win all the battles? "[We] know it's not the weapons." Danny had established the leadership criteria for choosing leaders. Tank commanders and pilots were drawn from Kahneman's work as an army psychologist. It was only part of the answer Danny was looking for. That system remains the basis for leadership decisions by the Israeli's.

"The 35" were killed because of a decision about shepherds. It was assumed, since childhood, shepherds were not militarist and were therefore harmless. The issues, however, were not the same as they were in their childhood. Things had changed. They were soon to be officially at war with Arab nations. They were already at war and people—Jews and others—were being killed every day. A "gut" feeling was inadequate for a life and death decision. Danny found out that if you "remove their gut feelings their judgments improved (Lewis, 83)."

He became a Nobel Prize winner and is author of the best-selling book, *Thinking Fast and Slow*. The book spans his career of studying how people make decisions. He, and his longtime friend and collaborator Amos Tversky, challenged the long-held idea that human decision-making is essentially rational. Malcolm Gladwell said as much in his book. *Blink: The Power of Thinking Without Thinking*. We make snap judgments about people and issues. We believe they are rational, and they often are. They seem to work. We believe we are right much of the time. The centering theme of Kahneman's work, however, shows there are many ways distortions occur in the human decision making process. Human bias, intuition and experience account for many distortions of judgment leading to overconfidence. "The 35" were unable or did not take the time to process the world situation. It had changed. Israel was at war. Life was not the idealistic pastoral life of their childhood.

Kahneman and his collaborator, Amos Tversky, have been called the Lewis and Clark of the mind. Their story is told in the book, *The Undoing Project*,[1] by Michael Lewis (author of *Moneyball* and *The Blind Side*). Their conclusions about bias in decision making are especially apparent when decisions are made in uncertain conditions.[2] Kahneman and Tversy, professors in economics and psychology, were familiar with uncertainty and decisions made in crises. Both were part of the Israeli military forces. Both fought in Israeli wars. They were instrumental in establishing the program for selecting Israeli Defense Force leaders and commanders.

Decisions are part of everybody's life. Little do we suspect we are making biased or skewed decisions. We assume our brains work rationally. We believe "What we see" is "All there is." Books by Dan Arielly's *Predictably Irrational*[3] and Steven Levitt and Stephen Dubner's *Freakonomics*[4] point out the inconsistencies of human decision-making. Their research has been furthered and put into the popular book *Nudge*[5] about decisions concerning health, wealth and happiness. The point is, "What we see is *not* all there is."

Decisions are often made in uncertain conditions. Often it is in crisis. Abraham left his homeland, Isaac and his wife experienced famine, and Jacob experienced family conflict and fled into the desert. Elisha experienced the threat of Jezebel and fled for his life. Uncertainty was the case in the biblical book *Ruth*. The popular preacher of *The Old Fashioned Revival Hour* and founder of Fuller Seminary, Charles E. Fuller, called Ruth the "Cinderella of the Scriptures." The book of Ruth is a life story, a love story, a historical story and a religious story.[6] It is all of these and more in the short four chapters of one biblical book.

Ruth is about decision and destiny It is the story of an outsider that finds destiny. The path to destiny came in her decisions. If you are familiar with the narrative, you know the backstory. Bethlehem was experiencing a famine. In the midst of the famine, Elimelech made a decision to move his wife and family to Moab. The uncertainty of crisis is often where poor judgments occur and bad decisions are made. In the swirling events of the famine, in the confusion and perplexity of the future, Elimelech decided to uproot his family and leave the Promised Land. The famine was all Elimelech could see but it was not all there was.

Elimelech moved his family from Bethlehem to Moab, a flourishing kingdom just east of the Dead Sea. It was not a great distance. It was across the Jordan. Moab, however, was not the Promised Land. Moab was not Jewish. Moab was different. The Moabites were idolaters. Moab was an ungodly place. These were the people that came from the incestuous relationship of Lot and his oldest daughter. They, along with Edom, had obstructed Israel on their wilderness journey (Numbers 20:14) and had even hired a seer (Balaam) to curse the Israelites (Numbers 22-24). Failing the strategy of cursing them, they sent their women to seduce the men of Israel and violate their covenant with God (Numbers 25:1-2). In the ensuing judgment 24,000 Hebrews died. Years later the Moabites over-ran Israel and made them subservient for 18 years (Judges 3:14).

Elimelech took his wife, Naomi, and their two sons, Mahlon and Chilion, to Moab. He knew the stories of Abraham and Isaac. He knew the trouble they faced when they left the Promised Land. He knew they faced exposure to the demonic. He knew the promises of God involve certain places, at certain times and doing certain things. He knew the blessing of God had a time and place. He knew it involved where God had planted them. That is, in the Promised Land. Later Naomi says she left Bethlehem full. They were not destitute when they left for Moab. Perhaps they could have stayed in the Promised Land. They had at least one rich relative, Boaz. Nonetheless Elimelech took his family with him and left. Very possibly he left despite hearing cautions and warnings from enlightened counsel.

In the course of time Elimelech died in Moab. Mahlon and Chilion, his sons married women of Moab. They, in the course of time, also died in Moab. The three men left three widows: Naomi, Orpah and Ruth. After ten years Naomi heard there was bread in Bethlehem. Naomi decided to return to her home and family. The three of them, Naomi, Orpah and Ruth, began to walk together. The girls said to Naomi, "We want to go with you to your people (Ruth 1:10)."

This is a common family scene. When close friends and relatives leave after a visit they may walk along together or linger a bit with them.

Relatives and friends may accompany those leaving to the train station or airport. People may just go out on the porch and talk together not wanting to part from one another. They share repeated hugs, kisses and good-byes as they get their things together to leave.

Pastor Campbell's father accompanied his brother to see him off when he went into the military. Dads and friends, often, will travel a distance with their sons when they go off to college or to their first job. This is the picture of Orpah and Ruth walking along with their mother-in-law. They are on the road to Bethlehem. Their emotions are running high. Naomi has been the only stable influence of God in their lives. She is leaving them. They insist they are going with her.

Naomi understands. She "gets it" as we might say. She knows she is a widower. She knows she faces insecurity. She can only imagine what awaits her in Bethlehem after her ten-year absence. She knows that her foreign daughters-in-law will face an even more uncertain life. As foreigners they could very possibly face danger and rejection in Israel and Bethlehem.

Naomi turned to her daughters-in-law and challenged their decision to leave Moab. She tests their resolve. She confronts their decision to go with her. She explains plainly there is no security in following her to Bethlehem. Naomi is past childbearing age. She cannot provide these young widows with husbands. Besides, even if it were possible, she says, "would you wait for them till they were grown? Would you restrain yourselves from having husbands (Ruth 1:12-13)?" Naomi paints an impossible scenario for her daughters-in-law.

All three of these widows knew they were disenfranchised persons in their societies. Widows were not employable persons in Middle Eastern culture. A woman's worth and security were wrapped up in having a husband. Any security they might have would be with their home and family. Their protection, provision and security would only be found with family.

Orpah's resolve was challenged and she kissed Naomi and turned back to her family in Moab. Importantly, Orpah's faith and future were challenged. Commitments, especially concerning faith and the future, are always challenged. Naomi's analysis of the future was essentially correct for her time and place. She was probably right in the natural view of things. It fit the logic and rationale of the Middle Eastern world. The natural viewpoint often seems hopeless. In the natural, things seem to be too difficult. Naomi says, go back home, it will be easier for you there. Your only security will be at home with your family. Naomi is in a faithless funk. She's saying, "Don't hang around me" "There's no hope here." "Things are far more bitter for me than for you, because the Lord himself has raised his fist against me (Ruth 1:13 NLT)."

What do you think went through Orpah's mind when she heard Naomi's challenge to go back home? Was she thinking that her mother-in-law didn't want her around? Was Naomi thinking she was a burden or just another mouth to feed? Did she feel the hurt of rejection rising up in her heart? Did she think, "You mean you don't want me?" Or maybe she thought, "There's no longer any place for me in Naomi's life?" We do not know what she thought or felt. But we do know that Orpah kissed Naomi and went back to her culture, her people, her past and her gods. "But Ruth clung tightly to Naomi (Ruth 1:14 NLT)."

Naomi again sought to persuade Ruth to turn back. "Look, your sister-in-law has gone back to her people and to her gods; return after your sister-in-law (Ruth 1:15)." But Ruth said, in reply, one of the most powerful statements of dominion in the Word of God. It is a statement that overwhelms the objections of the natural soul. It is a statement of dominion over the natural view of life. It is dominion over the "What you see is all there is" attitude. It is a statement of faith. The Bible notes Ruth's reaction to her mother-in-law. Ruth said:

> "Entreat me not to leave you,
> Or to turn back from following after you;
> For wherever you go, I will go;
> And wherever you lodge, I will lodge;
> Your people shall be my people,

And your God, my God.
Where you die, I will die,
And there will I be buried.
The Lord do so to me, and more also,
If *anything* but death parts you and me." (Ruth 1:16-17)

Ruth's reply silences Naomi. It silences Naomi's sensible arguments. Ruth, in one statement, took dominion over the natural events and silenced the voices opposed to her commitment. Ruth's statement is filled with absolutes. It challenges the natural world of relationships. It silences the counter-arguments of Naomi. Ruth seized her future.

Look at it. "Where you go, I go." "Where you live, I live." "Where you die, I die." "The God you serve, I serve." Rarely does one find this kind of clarity in a person's decision. A real decision is made of absolutes. They are absolutes you can and will live by. They are commitments you can build your life around. These are words that "pull down strongholds," and "cast down" arguments. This statement brings her thoughts into "captivity" and makes them "obey Christ." These words lead to destiny. This is this kind of decision that gives one dominion over the future.

This decision overcame the counsel of the ungodly. The counsel of thoughts outside of faith were cast down and brought into captivity—the captivity of Christ. What is the counsel of the ungodly? The ungodly say, "Live as if it matters what people think of you." It says, "Live as if the outcomes of your life are on your shoulders and you control them." The ungodly often obsess over the future. They fear lack and fear loss. The counsel of the ungodly says, "Live as if aging is something to worry about." Be sure and get hundreds of thousands of dollars in life insurance. The wisdom of the ungodly says, "Live as if satisfying your desires is central to your well-being and wisdom."

Decisions by others put Ruth in a difficult position. Decisions outside of her control seemed to put her life in jeopardy. This is often the case. How you process these things is critical to your future. Her decision brought her to a place of destiny. Her decision opened the world of God to her. Think of what her decision gave her. She became a key figure in the house of David. She became an ancestress of Jesus Christ. She became an instrument of God blessing her people and the nations.

Dominion is personal. Opposition and challenge often come from those closest to you. In Ruth's case it was Naomi. Her mother-in-law gave her no encouragement, no hope and stirred no faith. Naomi must have been the key figure in her faith. Ruth said, "Your God will be my God." No doubt Naomi was a critical influence when Ruth lost her husband. Emotions are deeply involved in moments of crisis. Feelings powerfully affect both Ruth and Orpah in their decision. To both Orpah and Ruth circumstances probably seem overwhelming and frightening. Ruth understands there is more than what can be seen. Decisions must be framed in faith. In the greatest crisis of Ruth's life she makes the decision that makes her a woman of destiny. She would not become just another figure forgotten in the pages of time.

There are many in the world and in the church that are like Orpah. They have the same emotions, affections and feelings Orpah displayed. They talk of love and especially of their love for God. They are so self-convinced of their relationship with God they will revile you if you intimate they are less than genuine. Orpah would contend with you if you challenged her degree of love and commitment to Naomi. If you intimate they are not as committed as they could be (or maybe should be), they will rise up in arrogance and pride claiming they are as "good a Christian" as anyone else—especially you.

The contrast between Ruth and Orpah isn't seen in the mundane events of life. The difference becomes apparent only in the test of hard times. The difference between a kiss and good-bye or a cleaving and refusal to go back to the world and its gods is made real in crisis. When the rush of enthusiasm is over, and the real facts are presented the question of following Christ or following the world becomes real. And the decision becomes the difference between destinies.

Dominion is an internal thing. It is a condition of the soul. It is the reality of a soul up to date with God. We know God framed the world for faith. Dominion is about framing your world in faith

Ruth's decision was something that moved beyond her feelings and what appeared to be natural or normal. To go with Naomi might even have appeared to be insane. It might have appeared far from reasonable. Dominion is when you make decisions beyond the realm of the flesh. Dominion is when you make decisions that overwhelm the natural and cast down the strongholds of the mind. Dominion is the place of destiny and where you find God.

Dominion is tested, tested, tested. Naomi says, "Go with your sister." The crowd says, "Be popular." The crowd says, "Be accepted, go along with everyone else." The crowd says, "Follow or you'll live alone." The battle is waged against words and thoughts to silence your commitment. The demonic agenda is to silence your testimony for God! It is to silence you. The demonic strategy is to remove your witness, your testimony, your enthusiasm for God from those around you. The strategy is to nullify or make void your dominion. But Ruth's words silence the opposing demonic voices.

This dynamic of the mind is what drives and gives force to the admonition in 2nd Corinthians.

> For the weapons of our warfare are not carnal but mighty in God for pulling down strongholds, 5 casting down arguments and every high thing that exalts itself against the knowledge of God, bringing every thought into captivity to the obedience of Christ. (2 Corinthians 10:4-5)

The Phillips translation paraphrases it:

> The truth is that, although of course we lead normal human lives, the battle we are fighting is on the spiritual level. The very weapons we use are not those of human warfare but powerful in God's warfare for the destruction of the enemy's strongholds. Our battle is to bring down every deceptive fantasy and every imposing defence [sic] that men erect against the true knowledge of God. We even fight to capture every thought until it acknowledges the authority of Christ.

Eugene Peterson's *The Message* puts it plainly.

> The tools of our trade aren't for marketing or manipulation, but they are for demolishing that entire massively corrupt culture. 5 We use our powerful God-tools for smashing warped philosophies, tearing down barriers erected against the truth of God, fitting every loose thought and emotion and impulse into the structure of life shaped by Christ.

Ruth's response literally casts down the false. In the test of her decision and commitment she casts down the strongholds of the natural mind and brings her thoughts to a place where she can "structure (frame)" her life in truth. When she says nothing but "death" shall separate us, she is speaking dominion.

Dominion language is what Jesus used in the wilderness temptations. When Jesus was finished answering—three tests specifically aimed to destroy the totality of Jesus ministry—Satan departed. Satan and the demonic were silenced. They had to find other times and occasions to test the resolve of Jesus.

Naomi can be seen as a picture of the human mind. Life is processed in the mind. There is a confluence of the events, emotions, successes or failures in your mind. In Naomi they all come together and say, "run away." Go ahead and "quit." The world says, "You have nothing to offer". That is what Naomi did. She consented and followed along when her husband in a tough time of famine ran from the place of God's choice. When she fell to being a widow in a foreign land, she ran again.

Dominion is always challenged. Think of the mind of Paul and how he processed life's events.

> I am more: in labors more abundant, in stripes above measure, in prisons more frequently, in deaths often. 24 From the Jews five times I received forty stripes minus one. 25 Three times I was beaten with rods; once I was stoned; three times I was shipwrecked; a night and a day I have been in the deep; 26 in journeys often, in perils of waters, in perils of robbers, in perils of my own countrymen, in perils of the Gentiles, in perils in the city, in perils in the wilderness, in perils in the sea, in perils among false brethren; 27 in weariness and toil, in sleeplessness often, in hunger and thirst, in fastings often, in cold

and nakedness— 28 besides the other things, what comes upon me daily: my deep concern for all the churches. 29 Who is weak, and I am not weak? Who is made to stumble, and I do not burn with indignation? (2 Corinthians 11:23-29)

Paul is recounting his many decisions. These decisions brought him to dominion. The false ministers in Corinth were trying to silence his voice. Paul's decisions silenced the opposition. They challenged his apostleship and ministry. He silences their rejection. He silences their opposition to him, the founding father of the church. Paul had authority to speak into the church.

The war in your mind is decided when you decide. You are not a donkey. When the allies put aside their politics and decided to invade France, WWII was really decided. When they decided to commit all of their resources, the war was decided. When they put their decision into action, the war was decided. The powerful truth of human personality is decisions of the will bring the mind along. Your mind must abide by decisions of your will in life. When the issue of your will—what you are *going to do*—has been made, the issue is settled. The craziness of the mind stops. You will be in turmoil until you settle what you are going to do.

At salvation the Campbell's decided to be as Christian as they possibly could. They were new creations in Christ and decided to make Jesus the reality of their life. "It is what we are going to do," they said. "We are going to be in church when the doors are open." It meant driving home from his midnight job and getting ready and going to church. It meant leaving the evening service and driving to work so he would not miss his shift. It meant not missing work and not missing church. And it meant many other things as well. The decision meant they would change and act like Christians. It meant giving tithe and other forms of support for the church. It meant changing and treating people right. The decision settled the issue. It removed all turmoil from their mind.

The decision of the will removes the power of Leviathan to twist emotions. No longer would the past dictate and rule their lives. The mind and emotions had to honor the will. The emotion-laden thoughts had to honor the decision. Thoughts were brought into the captivity of Christ. Their life could then be structured in obedience with the right accompanying emotions.

Decision is where processing life becomes crucial. The disappointments you experience, the failures of people, the misunderstandings and offenses are all part of life. The old poem asks the question about the validity of your Christian experience saying, "You cannot have traveled far—hast thou no scar?" Jesus was not afraid to show his scars. It may have been Sachel Page who said, "Love like you have never been hurt."

Ruth went to Bethlehem. In faith she went to a land that hates foreigners, and especially the Moabites. She cast down her fears. She served her mother-in-law. She asked, "Please let me glean?" She was unafraid to take a "stoop-labor" servant job gleaning for food. And she was unafraid to share it with her mother-in-law.

Ruth was a lowly gleaner. She was, in God, "glowing and growing." And we know her destiny opens. Boaz, Naomi's wealthy family member, notices Ruth. He becomes informed of the conditions of her life and her accompanying Naomi to Bethlehem. Hollywood would make her to be a stunning twenty-one-year-old beauty. She is, however, a widower that has lived a hard and exasperating life. Her hands are the hands of a worker. Her skin is the skin of one long exposed to the sun.

Her marriage to Boaz is a work of God's grace. It places her in the plan of God. She gives birth to Obed (meaning servant or born to serve). He is the father of Jesse, the father of David. She is the ancestress of Jesus Christ, of the house of David, the Savior of the world.

Think of Naomi. She left Bethlehem full and returned a bitter widow who claims that God had raised His "fist" against her. Think of the feeling she must have felt when she lifted the baby Obed from the arms of her daughter-in-law Ruth. Think of what she must have felt when she "laid him on her breast." She became a nurse to him (Ruth 4:16).

Can you imagine the tears of joy as the women around her said, "There is a son born to Naomi (Ruth 4:17)."

The book of Ruth is about decisions. They are crucial to dominion. Dominion apprehends the path to destiny. Dominion discovers destiny against all odds. Would you like to meet Ruth? Are there any questions you would like to ask her? So much opposition was in her life. But God orchestrated the steps of her life. She lived in faith. Her decision was to bring every thought captive to the obedience of Christ. "The 35" assumed, on the basis of a hunch, that it would work out. Ruth did not assume. She made an ironclad decision she was going know the God of her mother-in-law, Naomi. His name is Jesus.

A Harvard Business School professor teaching business models for innovation and success used the last class period to turn the theories back on his students. "How does business theory relate to you personally," he asked, with three questions?

> 1) How can you be sure you'll have happiness in your career?
> 2) How can you be sure your relationships with a wife and children will become enduring?
> 3) How can you stay out of jail?

So, how will you be happy? How will you have happy enduring relationships? How will you stay out of jail?

Raised in a Christian home he made a decision about Jesus at an early age. He was very successful in school and became a Rhodes Scholar. "The Rhodes Scholarships are the oldest and most celebrated international fellowship awards in the world. Each year 32 young students from the United States are selected as Rhodes Scholars to attend Oxford University.

As a Rhodes scholar he faced a very demanding academic and social curriculum. As a Christian he determined to set aside one hour each night to read his Bible and seek God for his purpose in life. His decision was challenged by the demands for study and involvement in the program.

But he did it. He said the discovery of God's purpose in his life came out of this commitment. He felt that without God's purpose his life would be misspent! That is, it would be a wasted life.

The soon to be professor, as a Rhodes Scholar, played basketball for Oxford. By working hard, they finished the season undefeated. His best friends were on the team. They made it to the British version of the Tournament Finals. The championship game was on Sunday. He had made a personal commitment and made it known to the team and coach that he would not play on Sunday. He talked to the coach and team. The repeated phrase he heard was, "You've got to play. Can't you do it just this one time?" Integrity—his personal integrity—became critical to him. This was the decision about doing what was right, or wrong. That's integrity.

He left the locker room and prayed. He had already made a commitment to God, but he had made it when there were no events like the finals. After prayer he felt quite sure that God said NOT to play. And he didn't.

Years later he wrote for the *Harvard Business Review*[7] and said, "it was a small decision." It involved one of several thousand Sundays in his life. He said, "Resisting the temptation, whose logic was in this extenuating circumstance just this once it's OK," has proven to be one of the most important decisions of my life. Why? "My life has been one unending stream of extenuating circumstances. Had I crossed the line that one time, I would have done it over and over in the years that followed."

He said, "The lesson I learned from this is that it's easier to hold to your principles 100% of the time than it is to hold them 98% of the time." You have to define who you are and what your principles are and draw the line in a safe place. It had led to happiness on the job and enduring relationships.

Why the question, "How will you stay out of jail?" For those of you who have spent some involuntary time in jail—did you have jail in the plan of your life? In the professor's class there were two who spent time in jail. This was a class of Harvard scholars and 2 spent time in jail. Jeff Skillings was a classmate at HBS. He is famous for the marginal oversight of Enron. A spectacularly failed corporation. When it failed it cost thousands of innocent people their jobs and sent Skillings to jail.

The professor adds, the metric by which "God will assess my life isn't dollars but the individual people whose lives I've touched."

Decisions are the path to destiny. They cannot be mere hunches or filled with "I hope so." They must be framed in faith. Decisions must be made in the crises of life. They must often be made in the face of extenuating circumstances.

CHAPTER 5

YOU ARE WHAT YOU SPEAK

It is hard for God to bless what you speak against.

Without dominion deliverance is vulnerable. Lacking dominion, one can again be ensnared in the past. Lacking dominion, it is possible to be trapped by the demonic powers that had once been cast down and thrown into the sea. Dominion is necessary to possess the Promised Land. And it must be possessed. Israel was free but they were functionally still a slave culture. What might the old mindset be in your life? What is your default mindset? What kind of thinking do you drift back to when discouraged or facing a setback or the unexpected in life?

Your spiritual authority or dominion can be measured by what you say. The New Testament book of James gives us an important truth regarding dominion. What you say—even if only in your mind—can accurately measure your dominion. Dominion is expressed through words. Your words reveal how much dominion you have.

Israel came to Paran on their journey through the wilderness. God told Moses to send spies into the Promised Land of Canaan. When the spies returned from their exploration of the Promised Land, an abundance of fruit and grain was in their possession. But they also brought words. They said, there are giants in the land that make us look like grasshoppers. They said there are walled cities to be conquered. The words triggered a cultural reaction from the old slave mentality. Ten of the twelve spies said, "We are not able," and "They are stronger than us (Numbers 13:31)." The people responded to the evil report with loud complaining and weeping all that night. They lifted their voices in complaint against Moses and Aaron. They complained that the Lord had brought them out of Egypt only to destroy them. They conspired to select a new leader over Moses. Joshua and Caleb tried to calm the revolt. They urged the people not to rebel. They knew the Canaanites feared the Hebrews. The Canaanites believed their gods had deserted them. The people of God, however, took up stones to kill Joshua and Caleb (Numbers 14:10).

Israel's behavior provoked God's anger. The Lord spoke to Moses and said he would disinherit them and make another nation greater than them. But Moses interceded. God relented of taking action but held them responsible.

> Then the Lord said: "I have pardoned, according to your word; 21 but truly, as I live, all the earth shall be filled with the glory of the Lord— 22 because all these men who have seen My glory and the signs which I did in Egypt and in the wilderness, and have put Me to the test now these ten times, and have not heeded My voice, 23 they certainly shall not see the land of which I swore to their fathers, nor shall any of those who rejected Me see it. 24 But My servant Caleb, because he has a different spirit in him and has followed Me fully, I will bring into the land where he went, and his descendants shall inherit it. 25 Now the Amalekites and the Canaanites dwell in the valley; tomorrow turn and move out into the wilderness by the Way of the Red Sea." (Number 14:20-25)

In one of the saddest turns of their deliverance they turned aside from Paran and back to the wilderness of the Red Sea. It was a death sentence. God told Moses, "Say to them, 'As I live,' says the Lord, 'just as you have spoken in My hearing, so I will do to you: The carcasses of you who have complained against Me shall fall in this wilderness, all of you who were numbered, according to your entire number, from twenty years old and above (Numbers 14:28-29)." All 600,550 would die in the wilderness. All except Joshua the son of Nun and Caleb the son of Jephunneh would die in the wilderness over the next forty years. They would not see or enter the Promised Land.

It is important to see the nation was turned aside by an evil report. They were not conquered by the forces of a stronger nation or by defeat in battle. They turned to unbelief after seeing and knowing the glory of God and his power. It had been displayed in their deliverance. An evil report, evil words, turned or twisted their minds. Their unbelief was expressed by their words. By their words they turned their deliverer's grace to anger. Because of their words they lost dominion. Because of their words they lost their destiny. What they could have become was lost because of their words.

It was not a rash or out of control dimension of God's character. Very clearly God says, "[They] have put Me to the test now these ten times (Numbers 14:22)." They have an adversarial relationship toward God. It was expressed in their murmuring and complaining, and in their adversarial relationship to Moses and Aaron. They attempted to put God to the test in their wilderness journey. One of these occasions was at Sinai in the incident of the Golden Calf. After receiving the Tablets of Testimony written with the "finger of God (Exodus 31:18)," God tells Moses to quickly depart from the mountain. God says, "For your people whom you brought out of the land of Egypt have corrupted themselves (Exodus 32:7)." God has distanced himself from the people. They are the people *Moses* brought out of Egypt. Over eighty-seven times God says *He* brought them out. But at Sinai, and again in the wilderness of Paran, God is ready to destroy them for rebellion and tempting his character and glory. What God promised at Sinai and again at Paran, He determined to bring to pass. They *will* perish in the wilderness.

When the mind becomes twisted it often finds expression in words. Words are spiritual and come from the heart. The children of God murmured and complained as they, no doubt, did as slaves. They conspired to replace their leadership. They accused God of falsehood in their deliverance from Egypt. It is true today. People delivered from their sins, addictions, lusts and perversions, when things do not go as planned or look difficult, resort to murmuring and complaining. They accuse God of being unfaithful by leading them into difficult circumstances. They become twisted when they do not see easy ways to possess the Promised Land. Like the children of God in the wilderness, people are often easily turned aside by evil reports and words. The turn to unbelief from faith is not because of overwhelming events and circumstances. The Lord said, "I have seen this people, and indeed it is a stiff-necked people (Exodus 32:8, *see* Numbers 14:11)."

How many refuse to enter the promises of God and are turned aside in unbelief. For the next forty years the nation wandered in the wilderness until all but two of those God delivered through the sea died. They died in the wilderness, they died in a barren place, they died short of God's promises. They died outside of the land God had prepared for them. They stumbled back into the wilderness because of words. At the place they could obtain the promises, their old entrenched worldview took over. It was a tragic end to a delivered people.

It is an important lesson today for all who are delivered. Dominion is not automatic. Dominion is not an event. It must be sustained. The old cultural mindsets must be "cast down," and "brought into captivity." Those old mindsets must be brought into the dominion of the new life, new mind, and new heart we have been given in deliverance. They must be held captive and made obedient to God.

The difficulty in Christianity is seeing spiritual truths. It is seeing how to activate or implement them in real life. That is the difficulty for many, perhaps most believers. When Bible truth becomes more real than the world around you, it changes you. Israel was truly delivered from Egypt and the hand of Pharaoh. They walked through the Red Sea with a wall of water standing up on both sides of them as they crossed on dry ground. The horse and its rider, the chariot and its driver and the army of Pharaoh drowned in the waters of the sea, but Israel escaped. Their world changed. They enjoyed and celebrated the reality of deliverance.

Once across the sea they gathered together as a delivered nation. They sang the songs of deliverance. They sang to the Lord.

> I will sing to the Lord, For He has triumphed gloriously!
> The horse and its rider He has thrown into the sea!
> The Lord is my strength and song, And He has become my salvation;
> He is my God, and I will praise Him; My father's God, and I will

exalt Him. The Lord is a man of war; The Lord is His name.
(Exodus 15:1-3)

They were truly delivered. But the demonic had entrenched itself in their minds. Their culture had been shaped by generations of slavery and social oppression. They had developed a mindset or worldview about how life works. Unless they cast down their old worldview about people, life, and God they would die short of their destiny. Even though they were truly delivered from Pharaoh, and the armies of Egypt could no longer touch them, they would perish unless the entrenched mindset of their old life was transformed. A new life was the opportunity God had opened to them. God opened it with their salvation. Unless a godly dominion was established, they would revert back and abort God's promises of destiny. The entrenched thinking and view of life in Egypt or the old life of the past would not work in their new life of freedom.

In a similar way, many believers today, delivered from their life of sin still live in the oppression of a spiritual Egypt. They enjoy and sing the songs of victory. They see their addiction, failure, bad marriage, threatened divorce, and renegade children changed because of their deliverance. They give testimony of God's power to deliver. They experience it. It is real. The question, then, is why sometimes after years of living in the midst of God's people and serving the kingdom of God, do they go back to the streets and back to the habits, addictions and oppression of their past? Or why do they fail to see the spiritual promises work for them? Why do they surrender to the demonic powers of their dark past? Why do they surrender and walk away from their promised destiny? Why? How does that happen?

The Hebrews at Sinai in the absence of Moses, and in the wilderness of Paran, failed to keep their minds against the twisting power of unbelief. It found expression in their words. Think about these statements. They describe the actions of this delivered people as they traversed the wilderness. They murmured. They complained. Being obstinately set in their mind it was too hard. They longed for the things of Egypt. They complained bitterly against Moses and Aaron. All of these words reflect the old life of Egypt. It is what slaves do. They complain. They complain about the tasks. They complain about their wages. They complain about the tools. They complain about the resources. These responses to life had become entrenched in their culture and hence in their minds and their speech.

We are the products of many sources. The nutritionist will tell you, "You are what you eat." And that is true as far as it goes. Some of us, it seems, become more than what we eat. But we are not just what we eat. We are not just what we can see. We are products of many things. It has been said we are like an old coat, it picks up lint everywhere. That is, from our culture. We all have many cultures that affect and shape our minds. Culture takes form as ideas within us. They find expression in the words we speak. We are born into a culture of family and relatives. We have cultures at school, in the neighborhood and with friends. They all have their languages and worldview. Amazingly we come to a place where we think we know everything and are certain of the things in life. Opinions and ideas are things we become *certain* about. They form our worldview and our foundational mindset in life. What we see is not all there is to reality. Our experiences are only a sliver of reality—they are not the whole of it.

Often people come to their pastors or leaders and say, "I'm doing everything I know to do, and it's not working." They say they are not being delivered from a problem, or their marriage is not working, or they are not getting ahead. A powerful insight came when a young pastor complained that he was doing everything he knew to do but the church was shrinking. He had recently taken over a church but it was declining. He said he was outreaching, praying, giving, preaching and doing all he knew to do but the church kept declining. His pastor was curious and said, "How does your wife feel about all of this." He said she hated it all. She hated the city, the ministry, the people, and just about anything else you could think of.

Pondering this, the pastor concluded, "It is hard for God to bless what you speak against." This is true personally and it is true where you have influence. Is it possible the words of people with influence, like a wife or leader, are hindering what God desires to do? Their words are hindering while they are doing all the right actions and activities. Could it be something happening in your life or ministry? Are words hindering God's blessing? Are your words hindering God? The Psalmist, in a lengthy contemplation, says Israel, "Flattered Him [God] with their mouth, [a]nd they lied to Him with their tongue (Psalm 78:36)." Then, later the Psalmist says, "Yes, again and again they tempted God, [a]nd limited the Holy One of Israel (Psalm 78:48)." I wonder how much of the limitation was linked to their words? Was it murmuring and complaining?

Consider what James says. "If we do not stumble in word," he says, "The same is a perfect man" and he is able to "bridle" or "control" his whole body. That's dominion. And for James, dominion is exercised and demonstrated by the words you speak. Dominion can be measured. It is measurable by the exercise of the tongue. It is measureable by the words you speak and language you use. The aim, then, of the demonic realm is to get you to stumble in your words. You can lose dominion and destiny by the words you speak.

In his unregenerate past, Pastor Campbell and one of his friends got in a fight. His friend, Campbell says, was of no use. Pastor Campbell stumbled and got himself wedged against a car bumper where he couldn't defend himself. He was beaten up. Seriously, beaten up. His lips were swollen, and his eyes blackened. He was, by his own confession, a mess. When he got home his wife laughed. She then tried to pry his eyes and lips open. Getting you to stumble is the tactic of the devil. The strategy of hell is to get one to stumble into a place of vulnerability. Many fights would not occur if someone would shut-up. Many delivered saints could live in dominion if they took care of their words.

Balaam's story is one about words. The fascinating and ironic events are detailed in Numbers 22-24. Many commentators have noticed the significance of these chapters in the recounting of Israel's history. It marks a turning point. Aaron has died, and the children of God have become a new generation. They have come along a route that approximates the Kings Highway from Egypt. Along the way the armies of Sihon and Og have confronted them and been defeated. They have come to the plains opposite Jericho. They are on the cusp of entering the Promised Land. Unknown to them, however, there is a spiritual battle in the hills overlooking their encampment. A war of words was taking place between Balaam, a sorcerer from the northeastern part of Syria, and the king of Moab, King Balak.

King Balak has been watching the nation of Israel. They have been transformed from a complaining and undisciplined group of refugees wandering in the desert to a youthful, powerful and organized nation. Balak and the elders of Midian are "sick with dread because of the children of Israel (Numbers 22:3)." They know the Israelites have handily defeated the Amorites. The Amorites had previously defeated Moab. Balak says, "Now this company will lick up everything around us, as an ox licks up the grass of the field (Numbers 22:4)."

The King of Moab and the elders of Midian agree they are in danger and send for Balaam. He is apparently a sorcerer or seer of international reputation. His spiritual blessing and cursing are renowned. They send a delegation to persuade Balaam to come and curse Israel. They said to Balaam:

> Look, a people has come from Egypt. See, they cover the face of the earth, and are settling next to me! 6 Therefore please come at once, curse this people for me, for they are too mighty for me. Perhaps I shall be able to defeat them and drive them out of the land, for I know that he whom you bless is blessed, and he whom you curse is cursed. (Number 22:5-6)

Deliverance to Dominion

The delegation brought their request with a diviner's fee to pay him for cursing the children of Israel. Israel is obviously a blessed people and too mighty for Moab. God went to Balaam during the night and asked about the people who were with him.

> So Balaam said to God, "Balak the son of Zippor, king of Moab, has sent to me, saying, 11 'Look, a people has come out of Egypt, and they cover the face of the earth. Come now, curse them for me; perhaps I shall be able to overpower them and drive them out.' 12 And God said to Balaam, "You shall not go with them; you shall not curse the people, for they are blessed. (Numbers 22:10-12)

The story is a familiar one. Balaam refuses to go because God told him in the night not to go. Balak sends another delegation with greater promises of wealth for his divination and curse. Balaam again refuses but invites the emissaries to spend the night. God again speaks to Balaam in the night with a warning to speak only the words God puts in his mouth. The next day he goes with them to curse the people of God.

On the journey God continues to deal with Balaam. As he rides his donkey, the poor beast, first departs from the road into the vineyards, then veers into a wall along the path and bruises Balaam's leg and finally in a narrow defile the donkey sits down. Each time Balaam beats the beast into submission. At last God does two things. First, God opens the beast's mouth. The donkey questions Balaam's understanding and loyalty because he has never done evil before. Secondly, God opens Balaam's eyes. Standing in the pathway, blocking his passage, was the Angel of the Lord with a drawn sword. Three times the Angel of the Lord had stood opposing the passage of Balaam to Moab. Each time causing the donkey to swerve to the side and avoid the drawn sword.

Balaam is on his way to speak words against Israel. He is going to curse the people of God. The angel then speaks to Balaam.

> Why have you struck your donkey these three times? Behold, I have come out to stand against you, because your way is perverse [twisted] before Me. The donkey saw Me and turned aside from Me these three times. If she had not turned aside from Me, surely I would also have killed you by now, and let her live. (Numbers 22:32-33)

The angel says that Balaam has taken a reckless or twisted path. He is "twisted" in his thinking. He is recklessly pursuing his quest for gain. God, however, has set boundaries over the words Balaam can speak. This is a spiritual battle. Balaam's thinking is twisted. Indeed, the donkey saw it. Balaam is now in a tight spot. The words of Balaam, the words of God and the words of the king are in conflict. Balaam is twisted in the middle. He was recklessly heading for a collision.

The Angel of the Lord was standing ready to kill the sorcerer. Balaam was a famous person with words. Now, the Lord is pressing upon Balaam's twisted mind how spiritually important words are. God is willing to kill him over what he speaks. The angel is not simply preventing Balaam from going but also giving notice or warning him about what he is to say. What Balaam says is literally life or death to Balaam. Jesus said, "The words that I speak to you are spirit, and they are life (John 6:63)." Words are spiritual. Proverbs puts it, "Death and life are in the power of the tongue (Proverbs 18:21)." The issue so many miss is the spiritual dynamic of words. They carry spiritual power. They carry power to bless or curse. Too often people operate without understanding of how to activate faith in their life. Often, they fail to see what they speak is spiritual and affects the spiritual world.

What did God accomplish with the donkey and the angel? Balaam said, "I have sinned." He says he has missed the right path. Balaam is going to say words, but they will only be those that God puts in his mouth. He has been hired to pronounce against the children of Israel. He carefully explains to Barak that he cannot go beyond what God puts in his mouth. He cannot curse because God has blessed.

A curse is a proclamation or declaration. It is a spiritual pronouncement that is aimed to impact the natural world. King Barak wants to shift the balance of power. He and Balaam know it is a spiritual battle. It is a battle won or lost by words—blessing or cursing.

In the midst of this narrative are some of the greatest promises to Israel and believers. Balaam gives what is generally viewed as three oracles while he is with Barak. All three oracles pronounce blessing on

Israel. In the second oracle Balaam utters a powerful statement of divine grace applicable to believers. Believers often quote it today.

> He has blessed, and I cannot reverse it.
> 21 "He has not observed iniquity in Jacob,
> Nor has He seen wickedness in Israel.
> The Lord his God is with him,
> And the shout of a King is among them.
> 22 God brings them out of Egypt;
> He has strength like a wild ox.
> 23 "For there is no sorcery against Jacob,
> Nor any divination against Israel.
> It now must be said of Jacob
> And of Israel, 'Oh, what God has done!'
> (Numbers 23:20-23)

Balaam spoke these words because God put them in his mouth. They are far from being a curse. Rather they are the way God views his people. Many believers quote these verses with little real understanding of their actual power. They are not ritual prayers. They tell us the power and importance of a believer's words.

Listen, again, "It is difficult for God to bless what you speak against."

Israel was on the cusp of entering the Promised Land. At this important juncture in Israel's history, Balaam, greedy for gain wanted to curse them. Balaam was aiming at speaking against the very thing God wanted to do. God wanted to give Israel the Promised Land. God wanted them to enter into their destiny. And God was willing to kill Balaam if he spoke against the people God had blessed. God would allow no divination or sorcery against them. In the first two oracles Balaam practiced his sorcery and divination while the king watched. In the third oracle Balaam simply faced into the wilderness with no articles of divination or sorcery and waited. The Spirit of God came upon him and Balaam spoke. He not only continued to bless God's people but also spoke of the future. He spoke of the promise to Abraham, Isaac and Jacob and of Israel's coming king. He also spoke of Moab's demise in the future. When he finished he left King Barak.

Curses involve words. Jesus came to a barren fig tree and cursed it saying, "Let no one eat fruit from you ever again (Mark 11:14)." The next day Peter saw it, marveled, and said, "Rabbi, look! The fig tree which you cursed has withered away (Mark 11:21)." It had dried up from the roots (Mark 11:20). The first curses in history were when God cursed the serpent (the other talking animal in the Bible), the woman, and the man. Later, Noah cursed his son Canaan saying, he would be a servant of servants to his brothers (Genesis 9:25). The great promise of God to Abraham includes curses:

> I will bless those who bless you, And I will curse him who curses you; And in you all the families of the earth shall be blessed. (Genesis 12:3)

Jacob cursed his sons Simeon and Levi because in their self-will they conspired and killed Hamor, the prince of the country, his son Shechem and all the men of the city. Jacob says, "Cursed be their anger, for it is fierce; And their wrath, for it is cruel! I will divide them in Jacob [a]nd scatter them in Israel (Genesis 49:6-7)." Shimei maliciously cursed David as he fled from Jerusalem in Absalom's rebellion (2 Samuel 16:5-6).

The Old Testament ends in Malachi. It is generally accepted that God did not openly speak to Israel for the next 400 years. The issues are multiple and include forsaking the covenant of God, betraying the covenant of marriage and fidelity to one another. In Malachi, God pronounces two curses.

> "I will send a curse upon you, And I will curse your blessings. Yes, I have cursed them already, Because you [the priests] do not take it [seriously] to heart. (Malachi 2:2)

> "Will a man rob God? Yet you have robbed Me! But you say, 'In what way have we robbed You?' In tithes and offerings. 9 You are cursed with a curse, For you have robbed Me, Even this whole nation." (Malachi 3:8-9)

In the first case the priests are cursed "already" and in the second case the nation is cursed.

In the New Testament, Paul curses a false prophet, Elymas, who was hindering his witness to a proconsul.

> O full of all deceit and all fraud, you son of the devil, you enemy of all righteousness, will you not cease perverting the straight ways of the Lord? 11 And now, indeed, the hand of the Lord is upon you, and you shall be blind, not seeing the sun for a time. (Acts 13:9-12)

Words are spiritual. This is supernatural. It's popular today to run life "by the metrics." The words we speak are beyond the metrics. Our words have spiritual impact in our lives. They impact the lives of others. Our words are able to move God. Think about it. Prayers are words.

To stumble in word—similar to stammer or stutter—means to lose control. Just like the physical reality of stumbling means a loss of control, to stumble in word is to lose control and perhaps destiny. The demonic world wants to put its words into the vocabulary of the redeemed and change the course of their life.

In James words and the tongue are put in the midst of a theological controversy. The issue is about faith and works. To "stumble" in one point of the law, James says, is to be guilty of all. He is talking about sin. Similarly, to stumble in word is about sin. In a fight, a shoot out, or a fire-fight, to stumble can be fatal. This is equally true in spiritual warfare. The Roman period of the New Testament was one of conquests. The Roman army conquered the world and left Alexander the Great weeping that there were no more worlds to conquer. Instrumental in Rome's conquest of the world was their military strategy, the leadership of Alexander the Great and the Roman soldier's armor.

Ephesians 6 describes the Roman armor. One of the crucial elements was the Roman "short-sword." Warfare often became hand-to-hand. This valuable weapon, the Roman short sword, was especially effective when your enemy would stumble. The encouragement of Paul to the Ephesians was to "stand" against the wiles and devices of the devil.

If you have ever been in a fight you know, as Pastor Campbell discovered, it is horrible to go down. You must stand. You must remain on your feet. Once you are down the fight is over. Then, the fight is not about winning. It becomes nothing more than a fight for survival. Escaping with your life is a victory, sort of, anyway. Much of the pastoral battle is waged with words. A tongue that is out of control or that is filled with the language of the old life can quickly undo a world of good.

The demonic desires your life and especially your tongue. "Life sucks" was seen emblazoned on a T-shirt. In other words, "Life's not worth living." That and many such words come across the un-tamed tongue and are broadcast to the world by those who cannot or won't process their life in godliness. Conversations full of blame are common. People blame their circumstances, they blame parents, they blame their health, they blame their money or lack of it, and almost anything else can be blamed for their troubles. Rarely do people see their situation as a lack of dominion. And rarely do they see the impact of their own words as casting and shaping their future. People generally see their circumstances as the cause of their stumbling. They are quick to blame someone or something.

The biblical admonition is to establish the life of faith through diligence and care. Peter gives a list and urges growth in faith so we never "stumble" or become unfruitful.

> Therefore, brethren, be even more diligent to make your call and election sure, for if you do these things you will never stumble; 11 for so an entrance will be supplied to you abundantly into the everlasting kingdom of our Lord and Savior Jesus Christ.
> (2 Peter 1:10-11)

The greatest prophet born of a woman, John the Baptist, stumbled over the ministry of Jesus. He told his disciples to go and ask Jesus, "Are You the Coming One, or do we look for another (Matthew 11:3)?" Jesus ministry was causing a controversy among the religious Jews. John believed the Messiah would gather Israel together and overthrow Roman oppression. Instead, Jesus, was causing division. John was offended and sent his disciples to Jesus.

> Jesus answered and said to them, "Go and tell John the things which you hear and see: 5 The blind see and the lame walk; the lepers are cleansed and the deaf hear; the dead are raised up and the poor have the gospel preached to them. 6 And blessed is he who is not offended [scandalized or made to stumble] because of Me. (Matthew 11:4-6)

Apparently, the works and reputation of Jesus scandalized John. Stumbling in these scriptures is related to the decision to believe or not believe Jesus. Clearly Jesus is the controversy of life. Peter made it clear in his first letter that Jesus will be the one issue in life.

> "Therefore, to you who believe, He is precious; but to those who are disobedient, The stone which the builders rejected Has become the chief cornerstone," 8 and "A stone of stumbling And a rock of offense." They stumble, being disobedient to the word, to which they also were appointed. (1 Peter 2:7-8)

The power of the tongue as a cause of stumbling cannot be underestimated. Proverbs 18:21 says, "Death and life are in the power of the tongue, and those who love it will eat its fruit." The power of words is one of the key issues in Proverbs. The Old Testament scholar and former president of Fuller Seminary David A. Hubbard says this verse in Proverbs occurs in one of three important sections in proverbs having to do with "Prudent Speech."[1] The characteristics of prudent speech are first, consistently blessing. Second, prudent speech must accurately report rather than spin or twist the facts for personal reasons. Third, communication requires careful listening. And fourth, prudent speech means asking questions to pointedly clarify the issues. Prudent speech results in 1) peacefulness, 2) fruitfulness (here in Proverbs 18:21), 3) riches, 4) freedom, and 5) acceptance. Hubbard points out the bookends of this section relate to the fool. At the head of this section in Proverbs is, "A fool has no delight in understanding, [b]ut in expressing his own heart (Proverbs 18:2)." And at the conclusion, "Better is the poor who walks in his integrity than one who is perverse in his lips, and is a fool (Proverbs 19:1)." Earlier in Proverbs we read, "He who guards his mouth preserves his life, but he who opens wide his lips shall have destruction (Proverbs 13:3)."

The deceptive power of the tongue lies in the fact that it is so small. It is seemingly insignificant. We live in a generation that is filled with words. There is a virtual tsunami of information in the form of words that descend upon us every day.[2] Every day 4 million new blogs are written and eighty million new Instagram photos are uploaded. There are 616 million new tweets sent into cyberspace. There are about 7,138 tweets per second and all are mostly words. It is an information age with over 3 billion internet users producing 2.5 gigabytes of data in 4 billion Google searches.

The tongue is small but filled with deadly poison. All of these millions of messages have an agenda. They are not mere "idle words." All of these words have purpose and aim. The tongue, however, flies under the radar. New babies are born and admired and commented on but only an unusual circumstance would cause someone to comment on the baby's tongue. They'll comment on the eyes, the hair, the nose, the smile and even the feet. But not really much is said about the tongue except when it becomes obvious the baby is "spitting up."

The tongue is a small thing but hear carefully what James says about it. James says the tongue holds an incredible place in the control of one's life and destiny. Notice, he says it is like a bit in a horse's mouth. It is small and largely unseen but through it a man who is much smaller can control the thousands of pounds of horseflesh and its power. Even a child is capable of controlling it. The same is true of people. The much smaller tongue is able to influence and control the whole of the person.

The tongue is like, says James, the rudder of a ship. Although it is relatively small and unseen it is able to turn large ships (James 3:4) through wind, current and storm. What you are saying in the storms of life direct the course of your life through the currents and winds of belief and unbelief. What you say about running away, about quitting and about "going through" are important in navigating and processing the circumstances of life. To control the tongue is to navigate during crisis rather than be driven by the currents and eddies of the cultural dialogue and narrative. Dominion is often about what you are saying when the battle rages. When the storms sweep down from seemingly nowhere and begin to produce cross-currents and swells of great waves navigation is critical. The tongue, as a bridle or rudder, steers the course to destiny. It steers the course to the Promised Land.

James says that words can kindle a fire. A word or two can spark something that can consume vast areas of life. California and Arizona, much of the western United States, and many areas of the world are susceptible to raging fires. A few sparks on some dry tinder can set the world ablaze. A few words misspoken on a dry heart can set it ablaze with anger or hatred. Words can kindle misunderstandings that separate and divide friends, neighbors, families and churches.

History tells us a careless toss of a cigarette, a smoldering lightning strike or unattended campfire has often erupted and caused thousands upon thousands of acres of forest to be burned to the ground. What was a small thing, only a smoldering ember, became a huge and uncontrollable catastrophe. A word that seemed a small thing can become the hotbed of controversy. It is seen all the time in the political arena, the courtroom and the church.

Is it possible to grasp what a few words are capable of doing? God has designed and set the tongue in our members with the capacity to defile or bless vast arenas of life. The moment the words are out of the mouth one's personality is set in motion to make those words true. God designed us so that all of our members are engaged when the tongue speaks. When you say, "I hate this one," or "I don't like that one," or "I don't think this or that is right," or "I know you don't love me," your whole body reacts to accommodate those words. Your body treats your words as truth. It becomes engaged to defend your words. This is the cause of many bar fights. Words said at the club got Pastor Campbell into a fight. Your body seeks to make your words a guiding reality for your life. Likewise, the words, "I can do all things through Christ," engage the entire personality in faith.

How many people really think about the words they speak? How many people really think about what they say? How many people really think about what they say to themselves? Prayer, you know, is about words spoken to God. Do people really think about what they are saying to God? Gossip and slander are words that engage the will and emotions of both those who speak and those who hear them. God has much to say about words and speech.

> Let no corrupt word proceed out of your mouth, but what is good for necessary edification, that it may impart grace to the hearers. (Ephesians 4:29)

In other words, there is no such thing as mere talk. There is corrupted and worthless speech that does not help, edify or exalt. God hates that kind of speech. In Proverbs 6:12, 14 God says, "A worthless person, a wicked man, walks with a perverse mouth ... perversity [crookedness, twisting] is in his heart, he devises evil continually, he sows discord." God continues—

> These six things the Lord hates,
> Yes, seven are an abomination to Him: 17 A proud look, A lying tongue, Hands that shed innocent blood, 18 A heart that devises wicked plans, Feet that are swift in running to evil, 19 A false witness who speaks lies, [a]nd one who sows discord among brethren. (Proverbs 6:16-19)

Notice, many of the things God hates involve words. God hates the lying tongue, the false witness and the sower of discord. Three of the seven involve words and the case can be made that the rest are accompanied by words. Words are spoken to others or within one's own heart.

Dominion is a sovereignty or right to rule your own life. God delivers. God gives the words of eternal life to your heart. You believe and confess with words to make salvation effective in your life.

> If you confess with your mouth the Lord Jesus and believe in your heart that God has raised Him from the dead, you will be saved. 10 For with the heart one believes unto righteousness, and with the mouth confession is made unto salvation. (Romans 10:9-10)

Do you see the place of confession in salvation? Twice the word confession is used in verses 9-10. Confession involves words. God follows in verse 13 with "For "whoever calls on the name of the Lord shall be saved." Again, calling involves words.

But deliverance is not the end. The Christian life is not merely an event. It is a life. Dominion is your right to rule when the powers of hell and the circumstances of life seek to steal your salvation from you. Deliverance is real. Dominion is real but not automatic. It is not guaranteed if you do not control the words you speak.

When Paul is making his case that all have sinned, he uses several quotes from the Old Testament. "Their throat is an open tomb." "With their tongues they have practiced deceit." "The poison of asps is under their lips." And, "Whose mouth is full of cursing and bitterness (Romans 3:13-14)." Human spirituality is seen through spoken words. If God wants to measure one's dominion, he can do so by the words spoken. If the demonic powers wish to measure the dominion a person has, they can also do so by the utterances of one's mouth.

Think of this reality. The issue is the heart. Because "out of it" are the issues of life.

> Keep your heart with all diligence, For out of it spring the issues of life. Put away from you a deceitful mouth, And put perverse lips far from you. (Proverbs 4:23-24)

The heart is the center of your moral activity. It is the controlling place of your personality and all you are. This is where morality, convictions, behavior and the issues of life have their source, their root, and their place of origin. Look at the connection Jesus makes in Matthew 12.

> Brood of vipers! How can you, being evil, speak good things? For out of the abundance of the heart the mouth speaks. (Matthew 12:34)

> But I say to you that for every idle word men may speak, they will give account of it in the Day of Judgment. For by your words you will be justified, and by your words you will be condemned. (Matthew 12:36-37)

The real impact of words will finally be felt at the end. The accounting comes at the end. Everything comes to an end. Jesus points to "idle" words. What are idle words? Are they words that are thoughtlessly tossed about in conversation? Are they words uttered without prudence that start a conflagration of destruction? Are they the words of those who cannot seem to stop talking? Are they words carelessly slapped on the social media pages and bulletin boards? Are they words that don't count at the judgment?

Carefully ponder the dynamic of words. The source and finality of judgment is about words. By words there is condemnation and by words there is justification. The contrast between a good man and a wicked man is their words. Both have over the course of life uttered countless words. The good person and the wicked person have vocabularies. The good man, however, takes good words out of his treasury and the wicked man takes wicked words out of his treasury.

> A good man out of the good treasure of his heart brings forth good things, and an evil man out of the evil treasure brings forth evil things. (Matthew 12:35)

Words "bring forth" the issues of life. By *words* the heart is revealed. By *words* the future is revealed. By *words* spirituality is revealed. By *words* dominion is revealed. Consider that! Words are what God says he will use to condemn or justify a person. God will consider your words at the end to condemn or justify you personally. Words are the material of depositions and testimony in legal judgments. This is true in human courts of law and is no less true in the eternal courts of heaven.

Think about the words you say about others. How would you react if they were said about you? Would you become livid with rage? Would you be filled with thoughts of revenge and getting even? Would you respond with words that carry even more intense emotional impact?

What if evil words were said about your kids? Would you declare war and take no prisoners?

Dominion is an issue of the heart. Much of the battle is over control of the tongue. Look at James 3 again. "The person who bridles his tongue is a perfect man." What a profound statement.

Dominion is demonstrated when you tame the tongue. Don't be deceived, the tongue's tendency is to gravitate toward evil. It is small but powerful. Its tendency is to fend for self at the cost of others. Humans find it easy to gossip and like it! It tastes good—like dirt when you were a kid. But you are no longer a child, and dirt still tastes good. We love the dirt on others because it makes our dirt look good. At least it doesn't look so bad. The statement commonly heard is, "Everybody sins." That supposedly justifies our sin. Have you ever been in a mud fight? Learn the lesson: you cannot throw mud without some of it sticking to you. One of the popular children's cartoon characters is *Peppa Pig*. The young pigs love to jump in muddy puddles. Of course, they are covered with mud after jumping in muddy puddles. People can be that way too. They love to jump into another person's mud. They cannot, however, come out clean.

No, your tongue is not full of love and grace. The Bible makes it plain that the tongue is a world of iniquity and it is set on fire by hell (James 3:8). It is something no man can tame.

The taming or bridling of the tongue starts with our thoughts. We think in words. We speak words to others but also to ourselves. We all talk to ourselves. Someone has said it is only dangerous when we begin to answer ourselves. Much of who we are operates in our heads. We hear the expression, "He lives in his head." This expression points out that our ability to function is associated with what we let happen in our heads. Our thinking is in the languages of our cultural baggage.

In 1st Samuel David is anointed to be king over the nation of Israel. But Saul is still the commander of the armies and controls the treasuries.

In addition to that, Saul hates David and has determined to kill him. David processes these things in his head or, as the Bible phrases it, his heart.

> "And David said in his heart, Now I shall perish someday by the hand of Saul. There is nothing better for me than that I should speedily escape to the land of the Philistines; and Saul will despair of me, to seek me anymore in any part of Israel. So I shall escape out of his hand." (1 Samuel 27:1)

His course of action, to go to the Philistines, came first in the words he spoke to himself.

The New Testament tells of a woman who was sick for years. She has been to the doctors and exhausted her resources seeking wellness. One day Jesus is passing by.

> And suddenly, a woman who had a flow of blood for twelve years came from behind and touched the hem of His garment. For she said to herself, "If only I may touch His garment, I shall be made well." (Mark 5:27-28)

She said to herself she could be healed. She didn't speak unbelief to herself. She said, "I shall be made well." Many do not say those words to themselves. They say things like, "I don't believe Jesus could heal me," or "I just don't know if God would do that."

The Prodigal wasted his resources doing what he always wanted to do. Finally, he had to ponder the consequences. He has almost became like the pigs he fed. To himself, he said,

> How many of my father's hired servants have bread enough and to spare, and I perish with hunger! I will arise and go to my father, and will say to him, "Father, I have sinned against heaven and before you, and I am no longer worthy to be called your son. Make me like one of your hired servants. (Luke 15:17-19)

In common language he determined the truth of his condition and a course of action to take. It took place in his head. It led him to a great reconciliation with his father and a destiny of wealth and dignity.

In contrast, the wealthy farmer with an abundance of crops thought to himself,

> Saying, 'What shall I do, since I have no room to store my crops?' So he said, 'I will do this: I will pull down my barns and build greater, and there I will store all my crops and my goods. And I will say to my soul, "Soul, you have many goods laid up for many years; take your ease; eat, drink, and be merry." But God said to him, 'Fool! This night your soul will be required of you; then whose will those things be which you have provided?' (Luke 12:17-20)

His course of action was determined by words and the story he told himself. His words led to foolishness and a rebuke.

In a similar manner the unjust steward considered his plight of being fired. He was removed from his position of power and in Luke 16:

> Said within himself, 'What shall I do? For my master is taking the stewardship away from me. I cannot dig; I am ashamed to beg. I have resolved what to do, that when I am put out of the stewardship, they may receive me into their houses. (Luke 16:3-4)

The steward's behavior began with words he spoke to himself. In Luke 18 a harassed and unjust judge:

> Said within himself, 'Though I do not fear God nor regard man, 5 yet because this widow troubles me I will avenge her, lest by her continual coming she weary me. (Luke 18:4-5)

He was moved to action because of the widow's words and the impact they had on his peace. His action was a result of words he thought in his head. So much of the spiritual battle for dominion takes place in the stories we tell our selves. How we process our stories and our memories is crucial to faith and dominion.

When we think of the Israelite's wilderness journey we see part of their problem was an unbridled tongue. Repeatedly they are said to murmur and repeatedly they stumble. They fall back to the old mindset. It is revealed in their words of complaint and resistance to enter into the promises God has made. What did they say? They said, "We are like grasshoppers." Joshua and Caleb were saying, "We are well able to take the land." Watching on the hills of Moab, King Barak was saying the exact opposite. He and the Moabite elders were saying, "They will lick up everything in their path."

We may be taken aback by God's statement, "no man can tame the tongue." People can spew out of their mouth good things and evil. They can speak words that are sweet like the waters of a refreshing spring and out of the same mouth words that are blasphemous, evil and destructive.

> For every kind of beast and bird, of reptile and creature of the sea, is tamed and has been tamed by mankind. 8 But no man can tame the tongue. It is an unruly evil, full of deadly poison. (James 3:7-8)

The scripture points out:

> With it [the tongue] we bless our God and Father, and with it we curse men, who have been made in the similitude of God. Out of the same mouth proceed blessing and cursing. My brethren, these things ought not to be so. (James 3:9-10)

And James uses the illustration of a spring of water. It cannot at one and the same time pour out two kinds of water.

> Does a spring send forth fresh water and bitter from the same opening? 12 Can a fig tree, my brethren, bear olives, or a grapevine bear figs? Thus no spring yields both salt water and fresh. (James 3:11-12)

Is victory possible? Did you ever think about the baptism of the Holy Spirit and having a new tongue? God could have chosen anything as a sign of being filled with the Holy Spirit. He chose to reveal his power from heaven in a "new tongue." Having this power ought to change you. The new life of Christ and the power from on high ought to bring about a change. The baptism of the Holy Spirit is not just another event. It is not just an item to check off on your bucket list of spiritual things to do. It should change how you think and talk. It is a new language. It is not the old language of the Egyptian slave. It's not the language of the refugee lost in the wilderness of sin. It's not the language of the Prodigal eager for his wealthy father to die. It's not the language of the self-seeking and unjust steward or the arrogant and wealthy farmer. It's not the language of the gang-banger. It's not the language of worries and insecurity. It's not the language of lust and pornography. It's not the conflicted language of Balaam. The Bible says,

> They have forsaken the right way and gone astray, following the way of Balaam the son of Beor, who loved the wages of unrighteousness. (2 Peter 2:15)

> Woe to them! For they have gone in the way of Cain, have run greedily in the error of Balaam for profit, and perished in the rebellion of Korah. (Jude 1:11)

Have you ever had the Holy Spirit scream to you, "No, no, no, don't say that?" Or, has the Holy Spirit whispered to you to "be still." How you respond reveals the spiritual condition of your soul. It reveals your dominion or lack of dominion over the flesh. In worship, in prayer and in fasting we gain dominion over the flesh. We are asked to pray in the spirit and with the understanding. Praise is an exercise of words that glorify God and put down the flesh nature. God inhabits the praises—words—of his people.

Dominion is intimately linked to the words we speak. It is linked not only to the words we vocalize but also to the words we think in our hearts. James, writing about faith and works concludes the matter by dealing with the tongue and our words. Without works, James concludes, our faith is dead. One's words reveal the heart condition. One's words are not just revelatory they are also determining of one's future. Control of the tongue is the evidence and exercise of dominion. You know whether you have dominion by your words.

Joseph C. Campbell and John W. Gooding

CHAPTER 6

SO QUICKLY TURNED

When life means nothing then things become your world.

A number of years ago Pastor Campbell and his wife Connie wanted to go to Malaysia. It was in their heart to pioneer. There was, however, another couple who also wanted to go. It was a couple with proven ministry and experience in Asia. The difference came down to money. The other couple had $10,000 in credit card debt. Because of money, they lost out on an opportunity and the Campbells stepped into destiny.

How do you think about money? What comes into your mind concerning wealth and possessions, financial gain and loss, using and spending money? What is your understanding of inheritance, the lottery, bonuses and promotions? If you suddenly came into a lot of money, how would it affect you? There is, perhaps, no greater challenge to dominion than money. How one thinks about and uses money are indicative of one's spiritual dominion. For many there is no greater need than dominion with their money. It is possible to have dominion in many areas—marriage, kids, emotions—and not have dominion in finances. Without financial dominion you will not become all you can be. One couple found a destiny in Malaysia. The other missed an opportunity.

God uses money to establish his kingdom on earth. In many churches there are flags—national flags—draped along the walls. At international conferences the flags of nations hang throughout the arena. These flags represent investments made in the foreign field. Each flag represents money believers and local churches have invested to establish works and workers in the world. God's people, however, are not the only investers in evangelism. The devil is also active.

Shortly after his salvation, Pastor Campbell discovered tithing. He saw envelopes at the back of the church and people putting money in them. He asked his friend what they were doing. His friend told him about the tithe. He told him it was ten percent of what they earned. Pastor Campbell was astonished. "Ten percent—that's nothing," was his comment. As an old partier it seemed a bargain. Much more than ten percent was often spent in parties and the other things he did as a sinner. His world changed.

Tithing was something that went beyond religion and religious activity. He understood Abraham tithed before Moses and the commandments. Tithe was established before Egypt and the Exodus. The tithe principle went all the way to the beginning when Abel offered a sacrifice that honored God. It goes back to the garden where God reserved a portion (the Tree) for himself. Campbell said tithing changed his whole outlook on money. He began to see money in terms of souls. He saw money as a resource for winning souls. He saw money was a tool for evangelism. He saw the demonic world also sees money in terms of souls. The demonic world uses money to promote sin. Sinning takes time and money. The demonic world uses money to divert and snare people.

Dominion is when you move the kingdom of God into your world. Jesus said, "When you pray," say, "Your kingdom come, Your will be done, on earth as it is in heaven (Luke 11:2)." There are two worlds running in parallel. There is a material world we were born into. The material world is not all there is. There is a spiritual world. It is unseen but like the wind it affects the material or physical world we live in. Our religion will have its roots in one or the other. David Wells, in *Courage to be Protestant*, describes religion as one of two streams.[1] One stream is human religion. It is self-made and carnal. It looks within to find God. It is based on human ideas. The other stream comes down from heaven.

Jesus was sent. He came down from the Father. God comes to us and by faith we enter that spiritual world. Faith says, "Christ in you, the hope of glory (Colossians 1:27)." The world's religion is from below. It is human and earthly. It is carnal, sensual and material. It must be cast down. Its thinking must be taken captive and made subject to the truth of Christ. Every disobedient thought must be punished (2 Corinthians 10:3-6).

Dominion is when God's kingdom becomes real in your life. Campbell, thinking back to the days before salvation says, "There is no comparison today to the life before." His life today is not just different—it is radically different. He says, piece by piece "God's kingdom has come into our lives." That's dominion. "You appreciate that. Whenever you choose to believe, God's kingdom becomes a reality in your world."

Recently Campbell was preaching a conference in Russia. There was a financial need. In the first few nights of the conference they received 320,000 rubles in the offerings. Campbell preached and took an offering. In one offering 3.2 million rubles (about $48,000) came in. What is the difference? Faith! You must choose to believe the things of God are more real than the things of the world.

The Satanic temptation in the garden was to turn Eve's heart to earthly desires. She was beguiled by the Devil. The Devil wants the desires of the material world to get in your head. The demonic desires you to exchange the dominion of Christ for the fruit of the world. The demonic wants the world's desires to be exchanged for your destiny, future ministry, and vision. Eve "saw" the fruit was desirable. What do you see in this world? The demonic looks for opportunity when you get a great paycheck. The demonic seeks opportunity when the paycheck is shorter than usual. It is important to control your brain and cast down desires, philosophies, and imaginations about money that come from the world.

"How do we measure life?" What makes life become, "The Good Life?" The demonic traffics in the material world. Luxury and ease have always been the Devil's lure. Laodicea was a great city in Paul's time.

In 2003 a visit was made to the archeological site of Laodicea during a tour of Turkey. The tour group walked across several acres of scattered remains, around a few fallen columns, and across a broken landscape with views toward Hierapolis in one direction and in the other, the site of Colossae. There was nothing much to indicate a great city.

Several years later we revisited Laodicea and archeologists had transformed the site. It provided a dramatically different view of the city. It wasn't just a few scattered ruins. Instead a reconstruction of the major finds showed the city had in former days broad streets, large theaters, and a hippodrome. It had been a truly magnificent city. Laodicea had a large Christian population in Paul's day. The apostle John, nearing death, wrote down the words of a letter from Jesus to the church there. Try and hear the words as they were read in the church.

> And to the angel of the church of the Laodiceans write, 'These things says the Amen, the Faithful and True Witness, the Beginning of the creation of God: 15 "I know your works, that you are neither cold nor hot. I could wish you were cold or hot. 16 So then, because you are lukewarm, and neither cold nor hot, I will vomit you out of My mouth. 17 Because you say, 'I am rich, have become wealthy, and have need of nothing'—and do not know that you are wretched, miserable, poor, blind, and naked. (Revelation 3:14-17)

This letter was to be read to the church. It was from Jesus to a church that had turned aside. Their value system was turned away from the heavenly and eternal. They were blind to the way God measures value. They measured their lives in the value system of material wealth. In their view "lack of want" was the measure of riches. They did not see the transient nature of the world's wealth. They believed they were well off. They believed they needed nothing. They were wrong.

> I counsel you to buy from Me gold refined in the fire, that you may be rich; and white garments, that you may be clothed, that the shame of your nakedness may not be revealed; and anoint your eyes with eye salve, that you may see. (Revelation 3:18)

God said repent and be cured of blindness. They needed God to be involved with their life again. They needed to turn back to God. They needed dominion over the blindness of the world's wealth to understand the true riches.

What does the demonic world desire? It desires far more than money. The demonic desire is worship. It uses the lure of wealth to obtain it. In the wilderness Jesus was challenged with wealth. The Devil took Jesus to a high mountain and tempted him with the wealth (glory: magnificence and splendor) of the world.

> Again, the devil took Him up on an exceedingly high mountain, and showed Him all the kingdoms of the world and their glory. 9 And he said to Him, "All these things I will give You if You will fall down and worship me. (Matthew 4:8)

Satan desired worship! Satan reveals his desire is for worship in Revelation 13. A beast is described—a demonic power—that will control the earth by controlling the money. No one will be able to buy or sell apart from the will of the beast (Rev 13:11-17). Worship will be controlled by the power of Mammon. The demonic promises wealth in exchange for worship. At the end of the age the Devil will mark people and by controlling their money he will control their worship. It is possible, as one of the end-time movies noted, you can have the mark of the beast in your heart long before it is on your forehead. Is it possible your money controls your worship today?

Walter Brueggemann is widely considered one of today's preeminent Old Testament scholars. His book *Money and Possessions* in the series, "Interpretation: Resources for the Use of Scripture in the Church," begins saying,

> The purpose of this book is to exhibit the rich, recurring, and diverse references to money and possessions that permeate the Bible....
> It [is] unmistakably clear that economics is a core preoccupation of the biblical tradition.

Brueggemann thought about titles for the book. It could have been something like, "Follow the Money," or "It's the Economy Stupid." Those tiles might work but did not seem appropriate for a sober theological treatise on money and possessions. He adds, that in ways that surprised him, he has come to the conclusion that the Bible is indeed about money and possessions. It is about the way money and possessions are gifts of God and intended to be used in praise and obedience to the Creator.[2]

To have financial success in life there are three specific actions about money to be approached in faith. They are first, faithfulness in the tithe; second, generosity in giving; and third, stewardship that includes saving. The tithe recognizes the covenant relationship the believer has with God. It is ten percent given from one's income. Generosity releases the miracle of return into the believer's resources. Generosity is rooted in the same word as fellowship. Generosity makes for fellowship. It is giving multiplied back to the giver as blessing. The third action of faith is saving. Saving is about stewardship. It establishes dominion over the consumer spirit of the world. It keeps one from therapeutic buying—buying things you don't need to impress people you don't know or like. It keeps you from the trap of "keeping up with the Jones's," or your brother-in-law.

America is a consumer nation. It has a consumer spirit. It is easy to see money as the source of happiness and security. But it is a deceptive spirit that twists the mind and subverts worship.

From the opening pages of the Bible and through many illustrations and statements we see how susceptible we are to money. Money is capable of twisting our minds and thinking to the point where we lose faith, make wrong decisions, and become emotionally overwrought. One man testified that he started stealing at age five. He stole from people he knew, people he had relationships with and anyone he could. At nineteen he was saved and converted. Immediately he was transformed and began to tithe. He began to see the worth and value of souls. Another person testified that he and his wife began to tithe but it was years before they discovered the dynamic of stewardship that brought blessing into their lives. He said it required the ability to say, "No." One man took pride in paying his bills as late as possible so he could earn a few more pennies in interest. He was not going to let anyone else use *his* money. He came to realize it was not really *his* money and what a poor example he was to those he owed money. He now pays his bills in a timely manner.

Following Eve and the first temptation in the garden a curse entered the world and the human race. It is the enemy of fruitfulness and blessing. In the process of time the curse began to work in humanity. In Genesis 4 it twists the mind of Cain. There are numerous ways commentators have written and commented about Cain and his offering.

Cain's offering was the result human religion. It was not revelation. In the Garden God killed animals—he shed blood—to cover the sin of Adam and Eve. Covering Adam and Eve with the skins of animals was for far more than to cover their nakedness. Cain had his own views about the cost of sin. Sin requires a sacrifice. It requires the shedding of blood. How we use and give money reveals our attitude toward God.

The biblical story of money and possession opens with Eve and desire. It takes on special importance for Israel and the people of God in Genesis 28. This is where biblical understanding of money really begins. Jacob makes a decision to honor God with a tithe. Genesis 28 is the continuation of the Jacob narrative. It follows Jacob's usurping—stealing—his brother Esau's birthright. Fearing his brother's revenge and with the little he can carry Jacob flees. He heads toward far off Haran. Exhausted, fearful and weary he does not enter the nearby city but lies down in the wilderness. Using a stone for a pillow he falls into an exhausted sleep. In the night he has a vision. He sees a ladder or staircase that ascends from earth into heaven. On it are angels ascending and descending. At the top, and over Jacob, stands the Lord. In the vision the Lord spoke to Jacob:

> "I am the Lord God of Abraham your father and the God of Isaac;
> the land on which you lie I will give to you and your descendants.

> 14 Also your descendants shall be as the dust of the earth; you shall spread abroad to the west and the east, to the north and the south; and in you and in your seed all the families of the earth shall be blessed. 15 Behold, I am with you and will keep you wherever you go, and will bring you back to this land; for I will not leave you until I have done what I have spoken to you." (Genesis 28:13-15)

When Jacob awoke, he declared:

> "Surely the Lord is in this place, and I did not know it." 17 And he was afraid and said, "How awesome is this place! This is none other than the house of God, and this is the gate of heaven!" (Genesis 28:16-17)

This event is loaded with meaning for Jacob, Israel and the children of God. The angels are the messengers of heaven moving in and out of heaven with messages and reports of things on the earth. Jacob declares this place to be Bethel—the House of God. Out of heaven, angels deposit things in your life. You never know what great thing God might do in his house. The idea of God's house was, as far as we can determine, unknown to Jacob. He had no doubt heard of God. He heard stories of God from his father and grandfather. It does not seem likely, however, that Jacob had ever personally encountered him. God said to Jacob, "I will be with you."

Jacob believed the word of God. It was a profound promise. It moved beyond Jacob and his immediate situation. It established a future beyond his understanding. God is *El Olam*. He is the God from Age to Age, the Everlasting God. He made a promise to Jacob that included his personal well-being, his future and the future of the nation that would be called by his name. A name (Israel) he will receive from the Lord at the Jabbok River crossing in the years to come.

Think of Jacob at this point in his life. He is alone, facing an unknown and uncertain future—maybe a short one. His life is out of his control. God meets him at night, in the wilderness and in a place, he calls, "The House of God." Jacob decided to respond to this astounding event. He believed God would genuinely protect him, bring him back to this land and provide for him. He also believed God would multiply his seed and give him the land upon which he had been sleeping. Jacob believed God. Faith leads to destiny, one he could not yet comprehend. Jacob believed God had a purpose for him in the world. Jacob responded by cutting a covenant with God.

The significant dimension of his covenant with God is the tithe. Malachi, the prophet that concludes the Old Testament, is conversant with covenants. The tithe represents a personal and national covenant with God. It means God's resources are involved personally and nationally. Malachi charges Israel with violating their relationship with God by infidelity, and stealing the tithe (Malachi 2:1, 3:8-9).

The tithe is a crucial factor in the believer's relationship with God. It is an action done in faith that moves God into the arena of life. It is ten percent of one's income. It is not merely a spiritual attitude or a hopeful wish.

Jacob set up the stone he had used as a pillow and made a sacrifice by pouring the little oil he had on top of it. He makes a vow:

> "If God will be with me, and keep me in this way that I am going, and give me bread to eat and clothing to put on, 21 so that I come back to my father's house in peace, then the Lord shall be my God. 22 And this stone which I have set as a pillar shall be God's house, and of all that You give me I will surely give a tenth to You."
> (Genesis 28:20-22)

This is one of the most significant statements in the Old Testament. Its profound truth continues today. Jacob made a commitment to give God a tithe of all.

Jesus makes it clear that there are two powers involved in money. One is the spirit of Mammon and the other is God.

> And I say to you, make friends for yourselves by unrighteous mammon, that when you fail, they may receive you into an everlasting home. 10 He who is faithful in what is least is faithful also in much; and he who is unjust in what is least is unjust also in much. 11 Therefore if you have not been faithful in the unrighteous mammon, who will commit to your trust the true riches? 12 And if

you have not been faithful in what is another man's, who will give you what is your own? 13 "No servant can serve two masters; for either he will hate the one and love the other, or else he will be loyal to the one and despise the other. You cannot serve God and mammon. (Luke 16:9-13)

The strongholds of Mammon must be cast down if one is to have dominion with money. The worldly view of money must be demolished. This is done by particular actions of faith. Financial dominion requires faithfulness in the tithe.

The most famous misunderstanding of wealth came during the Exodus. The Israelites, following the last of the ten plagues, "spoiled" the Egyptians. After the Angel of Death moved through Egyptian households the wealth of Egypt was freely given to Israel. Many have noted that it amounted to 400 years of back wages. In the wilderness, however, they abandoned hope Moses would return from the fiery mountain. They requested Aaron to "make" them gods.

> And [Aaron] received the gold from their hand, and he fashioned it with an engraving tool, and made a molded calf. Then they said, "This is your god, O Israel, that brought you out of the land of Egypt!" 5 So when Aaron saw it, he built an altar before it. And Aaron made a proclamation and said, "Tomorrow is a feast to the Lord." (Exodus 32:4-5)

Ponder how quickly they turned aside after their miraculous deliverance from Egypt. The gold they gave to Aaron was the wealth of Egypt. God had his own purposes for blessing Israel with wealth. But Israel, in their insecurity and fear, built their own god. They said, "This is your god." But gods are not made with human hands. Eighty-seven times God says in one form or another, "I am the Lord who brought you up out of Egypt." Their deliverance was not by a golden calf or the gods of Egypt. How quickly, they made their own image of security and wealth. God reminds them later:

> And you shall remember the Lord your God, for it is He who gives you power to get wealth, that He may establish His covenant which He swore to your fathers, as it is this day. (Deuteronomy 8:18)

Israel knew God and had seen his power. They and many others were not ignorant of God or his power. How quickly, however, they turn to wealth. People commonly see money, wealth and power as their security. They think these are able to deliver them from any difficulty in life. Money dictates many decisions in life. Where we live, where we work and how we worship are often money decisions. Dominion comes by actions of faith. Faith moves God.

Offerings are particularly revealing. We use money to honor God. Giving shows our attitude about money and God. This is true in every offering. It is not just *what* you give but also *how* and *why* you give. The offering reveals whether you serve God or Mammon. God allows no competitors. Offerings must honor God as he is, God.

Elisha's young disciple, Gehazi, in 2 Kings 5 had an attitude common today. He feels he must "run after the money." Gehazi creates a reason to leave and follow after mammon.

> But Gehazi, the servant of Elisha the man of God, said [to himself, in his own mind], "Look, my master has spared Naaman this Syrian, while not receiving from his hands what he brought; but as the Lord lives, I will run after him and take something from him." 21 So Gehazi pursued Naaman. (2 Kings 5:20-21).

When Gehazi returned home from Naaman with garments and money given him, he was questioned by Elisha. But Gehazi denied running after Naaman. Elisha said:

> "Did not my heart go with you when the man turned back from his chariot to meet you? Is it time to receive money and to receive clothing, olive groves and vineyards, sheep and oxen, male and female servants? 27 Therefore the leprosy of Naaman shall cling to you and your descendants forever." And he went out from his presence leprous, as white as snow. (2 Kings 5:26-27)

Running after the wealth of the world turned Gehazi into a liar. Gehazi created a need and then formulated it to Naaman in spiritual terms. Naaman had been miraculously healed. He offered to pay Elisha. The prophet refused his wealth. Money couldn't buy healing. Miracles are not purchased. They are gifts. Naaman's miracle came when in faith he obeyed the words of the prophet. Gehazi thought he could create a time and place for gain but brought ruin on himself, his family and his descendants.

In the New Testament there are two examples that reveal the seductive and twisting nature of Mammon. We know Judas sold the Lord for thirty pieces of silver. Also, following the resurrection the New Testament church experienced a dramatic turn concerning money and giving.

Ananias and Sapphira were members of the church in Jerusalem. Apparently, they had prominence in the city and church. The church was experiencing an outpouring of generosity and many new converts sold land or possessions and gave the proceeds to support the church. During this time Ananias and Sapphira agreed to sell a possession and give a portion of the proceeds to the house of God. However, they also attempted to deceive the church into believing they were giving the entire amount of the sale.

The story is told in detail in Acts 5:1-11. Peter confronted the duplicity of Ananias. Was the money yours and in your control, Peter asked. Then Peter said, "Why have you conceived this thing in your heart? You have not lied to men but to God (Acts 5:4)." Ananias died on the spot. This produced a great fear in the congregation. A few hours later the scene repeated itself when Ananias' wife, Sapphira, came in. Peter said, "Tell me whether you sold the land for so much?" She said they had. Then Peter confronted Sapphira about the truth. The truth is often found in the details. The questions of an interrogator establish the line of events, people, times, and places. Details uncover the truth. Then Peter said to her, "How is it that you have agreed together to test the Spirit of the Lord? Look, the feet of those who have buried your husband are at the door, and they will carry you out." She immediately fell and breathed her last. They buried her by her husband (Acts 5:9-11).

This is a stunning series of events. This event jarred the sensibilities of the church and people. Great fear fell on those who heard about these things.

You cannot escape the issues. First, deception about money had killed two people. They told an untrue story about their money. Has this ever happened to you? Have you fudged, cheated or told an untrue story about your money? Have you lied to your spouse, your pastor, your employer or to God? Second, lying about money is not just a lie to people, but also a lie to God. It is said that, "Money talks." In this case it certainly did.

Paul writes to the church at Rome, "Don't be conformed" to the world. Don't fool yourself with the world's wisdom. You are not nearly as self-made as you think or wish. Culture and cultures have shaped your life to a profound degree. It includes shaping how you think about and view money. God can deliver you in a moment from the world and bondage of sin. You can be saved. You can never be "more saved." Yet, biblically, you can be in need of transformation. We may be saved and yet still have hindering issues aligned with the world. The world's mindsets have their own language. Money (Mammon) is one of them.

The Gooding's had two close friends in a pioneer work. They were new converts and very active within the church. As newlyweds, the husband started a business and the wife worked at a local financial institution. The husband had been raised in a well regimented home with good income and regular hours. He, more or less—mostly more—expected the same in his marriage. The responsibility fell on his wife to create a home like his parents. His anger was not yet transformed and under control. If the household, including dinner, were not what he was used to, he would boil over in anger. Complicating the newlywed's new life was an absence of money. His new business was not making the money of his parent's home.

The financial pressure bled over onto his wife. It eventually moved her to embezzle from her job. Gooding's pastor did not want to deal with the issue when it became a matter for the law. So, Gooding and his wife accompanied the young wife to a meeting with the FBI. They helped negotiate a plan to pay it all back without jail time or other repercussions—she did lose her job. It was an eye-opener for Gooding to see the power of money to move people. These were not evil people. They were young, they were new converts, they were newlyweds and they had no clue about money. They were delivered and saved but they had no dominion over their money. They remained married and the husband adjusted his understanding about how much living really costs.

God tests, and the devil tempts concerning money. One of the greatest tests is when times are stressful and barren. In the Old Testament there were often times of famine that tested Israel. There was a famine in Bethlehem when Elimelech took Naomi to Moab. Other famines affected both Abraham and Isaac. During a famine, Abraham went to Egypt.

> Now there was a famine in the land, and Abram went down to Egypt
> to dwell there, for the famine was severe in the land. (Genesis 12:10)

Egypt represents the wealth of the world. It represents security and prosperity. There was, however, a cost in going to Egypt. He had to lie. Again, Mammon produced falsehood. Actually, Abraham made his wife lie. The demonic power of money will place you in a compromising position.

Abraham went down to Egypt. He came back with some Egyptian baggage. Hagar, an Egyptian maidservant, returned with Abraham from his sojourn in Egypt. Over time she grew into a woman in their household. Sarah, in her barrenness, offered her to Abraham. She became pregnant and gave birth to Ishmael. What you bring with you from the world will eventually become a curse. The wrong decisions in times of barrenness can live long past you and into the generations that follow you. The decisions of the flesh, unbelief, and desire, give immediate birth to trouble. Often, it is terrible and far-reaching trouble.

In the case of Isaac there was a famine and he went to the Philistine king, Abimelech. Then God came to Isaac, and said, "Do not go down to Egypt; live in the land of which I shall tell you. Dwell in this land, and I will be with you and bless you (Genesis 26:2-3)." In contrast to his father, Abraham, Isaac was obedient and remained where God told him. He "sowed" in the land and reaped in the same year a hundredfold; and the Lord blessed him (Genesis 26:12).

Sowing precious seed in a time of barrenness is a revelation. Ministry is released by sowing precious seed in barren times. Isaac invested precious seed and reaped the blessing of God. Jesus observed a widow give 2 precious mites to the kingdom. Her story is renown today. Another widow invested enough meal and oil to make a single cake. She received the favor of God. How do you handle barrenness?

Tithing is evidence of a covenant relationship with God. You have access to God's resources when he has access to your resources. God promises to rebuke the devourer and open up heaven's resources to pour out blessing on you. Tithing is a profound opportunity. The relationship you have with God affects every aspect of life. We often view money as our source in life. Dominion, however, is when God is our source. Practically, how you spend your money tells the story of your morals, your values, your lifestyle and your relationships. Without dominion over your finances you will be a wanderer and vagabond on the earth.

The story of Dr. Livingstone's goat is instructive. Traveling in hostile territory in Africa, Doctor David Livingstone had a white goat. He used the milk for his health. Traveling with a train of supplies he had been repeatedly attacked and stolen from. Robberies and runaways plagued his travel. He encountered a particularly powerful tribe that put his travel in jeopardy. He was told he should cut a covenant with the chief. He was told he and the chief or their representatives would cut themselves and then mix the blood in a drink. They would then make promises. If the promises were kept then blessing would come. If they were violated, they would be cursed. They would then exchange gifts. The chief wanted the goat and Livingstone was reluctant to give it. Finally, he agreed, and the chief gave Livingstone a large ornate spear. It did not seem right to Livingstone until he noticed that wherever he went the spear meant something to the rest of the tribes he encountered. Wherever he planted the spear in the ground the goods in his caravan remained safe and unmolested. He was in covenant with a powerful tribal leader and it brought Livingstone protection and blessing.

Giving is also a physical act by faith that involves the release of a spiritual dynamic. Giving is the key to reward and multiplication of blessing. Shortly after their conversion Joe and Connie noticed his old biker buddy, Billy and his saved wife, were living a blessed life. This was true even though they were making less money than Joe and his wife.

When Joe and Connie saw the greater blessing of people with less, they understood the need to sow seed for financial increase. They began giving beyond the tithe. Pastor Campbell was working for the telephone company when they began to establish area codes. One morning on break, he recognized the numbers in the new phone book to be published and distributed were all wrong. It was the grace of God that let him see what others did not. It established a new dominion on his job. God anoints for blessing. Prosperity is a supernatural dimension of God.

If you are ever to break the curse of poverty you will have to believe. You will have to move beyond what your financial counselor, check book and bank accounts say. What you see is *not* all there is. If you need money you must sow money in order to reap money. If you need love, forgiveness and grace in your home you must sow love, forgiveness and grace in your home. If you sow to the spirit you will reap of the spirit. If you sow to the flesh you will of the flesh reap corruption. Giving is the multiplication factor. Jesus says some will reap 30-fold, some 60-fold and some a hundred-fold. Sowing—giving—determines the magnitude of the reaping. You can see this in people on the job, in relatives, in friends and even in church members. There are good people with good and sometimes great jobs. They are often, however, in turmoil financially. They cannot seem to ever make ends meet. On the job they borrow from co-workers. Their stewardship of money is filled with bad decisions. When they get a raise, they do not save or use it for needs, rather they eat more or they eat more expensively.

In the early days of the United States—and from time to time since then as well—oil districts in America operated with a feast or famine mentality. When the price of oil was up then there was vast wealth to be made. When the oil economy was down the rigs and equipment were idle and the workers were laid off. Many abandoned the oil fields and looked for work elsewhere.

In the mining town of Globe, Arizona it was essentially the same. During a strike the miners were suddenly confronted with the realities of the economic world. Many found themselves out of work. Many were confronted with the reality that they had many goods, but they owned nothing. They had cars and trucks, houses and furniture, tools and toys but owned nothing. Many had charged the "company store" for their groceries and anything else they needed because they knew another check was coming. Their charges could be paid off. But in a strike or lay-off the check was no longer coming. Almost overnight, as the song says, "they owed their soul to the company store."

Blessing and curse are two common words in the biblical vocabulary. They involve mindsets about money. Like many today, the miners and oil field workers spent their money before they got it. Many today spend their income tax return or their bonus check before it is deposited. The sad thing is many cannot remember or point to anything they spent the money on last year, or the year before.

The wrong use of money can curse your finances.

Saving gives you dominion over the consumer spirit that is in the world. America is a consumer culture. It is a culture the rest of the world derides but wishes they had. The human soul is a consumer at heart.

The problem many have is realizing that prosperity requires sowing in the area of your need. This is the struggle. "I need money! You are asking me to give it." "You are saying I need to save it," or I need to be a "steward of it." "How can I be a steward over what I don't have?"

People often say, "How can I save, I barely make it?" Think about some things. Many companies match IRA or 401K contributions. Wow! They match your savings. That is a good deal. Yes, the government is always tricking the system, but it remains a way to save. Think about purchases. Do you ask how much interest you will be paying, or do you ask, "How much is the monthly payment?" Those are vastly different questions. So different are these questions that the government has mandated showing the difference on your credit card or loan statement. Paying the minimum means paying for a very long time. You will still be paying long after you no longer own, use or even remember whatever it was you purchased.

Look at what you spend your money on. One of the members of the church had a good job. He had been at it a career's worth of time and made good money. He decided to track all of his expenditures. His discovery? He spent far more money that he ever imagined on snack and lunch items at a convenience store. Did you know that $10-12 twice a day adds up to a lot of money? Another church member did two coffee runs a day. It was not just coffee she liked. She liked the atmosphere and fancy blends. When Gooding asked her about it in a discussion of "I have no money," she simply said, "Don't go there, Pastor." Obviously, it was not something she was about to give up until they were in the poor house and had no car to drive to the drive-up window.

So, where does your money really go? Do you insist on allowing your wayward kids to drain your resources for their crazy life? One statement was, "Parents no longer discipline their children. They just throw money after them." Is that you?

You must understand the enemy's weapons and strategy to live effectively for Christ. The Devil is a thief. Kill, steal and destroy is the demonic strategy. It is the demonic world that causes your money to evaporate or, as the prophet says, be put into bags with holes. The demonic says you'll not have enough or don't have enough. The demonic says you cannot afford to give. The essential statement Jesus made is, "you cannot serve God and Mammon." Yet, this is exactly what people attempt.

At Caesarea Philippi (the gates of hell) Jesus made a tactical statement about dominion. Jesus asked the disciples about who people were saying he was. Peter said Jesus was the Christ, the Son of the Living God.

> Jesus answered and said to [Peter], "Blessed are you, Simon Bar-Jonah, for flesh and blood has not revealed this to you, but My Father who is in heaven. 18 And I also say to you that you are Peter, and on this rock I will build My church, and the gates of Hades shall not prevail against it. 19 And I will give you the keys of the kingdom of heaven, and whatever you bind on earth will be bound in heaven, and whatever you loose on earth will be loosed in heaven."

Peter, Jesus says, has a revelation from heaven. They were standing in the midst of several pagan temples and the site of demonic fertility rites. Jesus gains the "confession" from Peter of who he is. "Who Jesus is," is the key to all Christian experience. Who is Jesus to you? It is not about what others say or believe. It is about your revelation of Jesus as your personal savior.

Then Jesus talks about building his church and the gates of hell. Gates are places of control, places where the road narrows and principalities establish tolls. They are where thieves ambush and steal. These are barriers to blessing and restraints on productivity. Gates represent attitudes and philosophies of friends and family. Gates can be culturally acquired attitudes about money and life. Sometimes gates are attitudes formulated from personal experiences in life.

Biblically, gates are places of rule and judgment. The virtuous woman's husband sat in the gate of the city (Proverbs 31:23). He had position and authority in the affairs of the city. In the gates (narrow and restricted places in life) decisions are made. The decision of Boaz to marry Ruth was decided in the gate of the city.

When you enter a gate or doorway you must cross a *threshold* that causes one to pause or hesitate before going through. When you cross the threshold, you enter a new arena. It is a new set of domains and authority. In Malaysia you can visit the Batu Caves and the moment you cross the threshold (the entrance) your mind and spirit understand you are in a place of demonic authority. Step across the threshold into the caves and you'll be spiritually assaulted. You'll likely feel nausea, blurring of thoughts or some other confusion of spirit. Step back across the threshold and out of the caves and things become normal. Spiritually we are confronted with these narrow places. These are strongholds, imaginations, arguments and vanities often concerning money.

We believe these gates are assaulted and blown away by God's power. All gates and doors are blasted open in the moment of deliverance so we can enter into God's blessing. That is rarely the case. Jesus says to Peter and believers, "I give you the keys." You open doors with "keys." If you unlock the doors of oppression with the keys of God, you enter a new arena of blessing. God's promise is that we shall possess the gates of our enemies.

As pastor Gooding was finishing his Master's Degree, the director of the seminary program interviewed him. This was something they did for all graduates. They wanted to make sure they did not graduate a nut case. Pastor Gooding did pass, by the way. After a cursory look at the academic record and qualifications he asked the question that he had probably wanted to ask for years. He had known Gooding was a pastor in a small-town church. He also knew there was a dimension of overseas ministry and church planting in the church. He asked, "How do you do all these things." He wasn't asking how physically fit Gooding was. He was asking, "How do afford to do all these things?" He was asking how the church could afford to plant churches, invest in overseas ministry, support evangelism and, it seems, even support a pastor.

This interested Pastor Gooding because the man asking was obviously employed as a professor of a major seminary. He was also the director of the Master's program. In addition, his wife was the pastor of First Presbyterian Church in Phoenix, Arizona. The church occupies two city blocks in downtown Phoenix. It had little or no expression apart from what the denomination could claim. Gooding's response was, "We ask people to give, and they do." There is no endowment, government subsidies or other financial program. People give to the things of God and are in turn, blessed.

Every revival is accompanied by great giving. Giving to world evangelism, to church planting and investing in souls produces a new crop of resources. This is true personally, individually and corporately. It really does come from people who, in the world's eyes, have little.

Dominion is when you act by faith and bring the reality of the kingdom of God into the arena of your life. Whenever and wherever you sow to your need God releases a supernatural dynamic into your life. Do you know, what you see is not all there is?

Do you believe what you see is all there is? In one testimony, a thirty-seven-year-old woman with spreading breast cancer was without finances, without insurance and facing ruin. But she understood that what she saw was not all there was. She decided to remain faithful in giving. She cried out to God who owns it all, including the cattle on a thousand hills. She was healed and the bills got paid. Faith and giving are critical key to blessing.

Again, the desire for the world is used by hell to control and manipulate lives. But the world as we know it is dying. The world is passing away. There is no future in the world.

Think about it. "Are you grateful for your income and money?" It is stunning when you drive through neighborhoods. You can tell the neighborhoods where people have worked, labored and invested. You can tell where government subsidies and entitlements have been invested. Entitlement does not naturally produce thankfulness. Are you grateful? Gratitude is a spiritual commodity.

Yes! You must tithe, you must give, and you must pay attention to how you spend and save it. Otherwise you cannot genuinely hope for dominion. A big winner ticket in the lottery will not give you dominion. Dominion is not really about an amount of money. It is an attitude. Poverty is not an amount of money. It is an attitude. In one church two roommates were similar in many ways. They roomed together and had similar jobs, bills and car payments. The difference was when they were asked if they could bring a dish to a fellowship. One always said she could, and the other never had the resources to do so. It was an attitude about money and giving that made the difference.

Pastor Wayman Mitchell, founder and leader of the Christian Fellowship Ministries, commenting to a group of pastors, said he looks for financial solvency in disciples. A minister must be able to handle and be stable in issues involving money and possessions.

Dominion in finances, like other dominions in life, happens when by faith you believe God. When you choose to believe God with actions you move God's kingdom into yours. It is a covenant relationship. It is not magic, not the lottery, not a wish. It is a reality of faith. This is true for many things. You move God's kingdom into yours by believing and acting on God's word. God promised that Jacob would return to his homeland. Destiny has your name on it. Jacob's father-in-law sought to hurt him. But Jacob's life was in covenant with God. God promised to be with him and kept Jacob secure from Laban's harm (Genesis 31:7). God will keep you and even open the windows of heaven's provision for you (Malachi 3:10-12).

CHAPTER 7

THE ALGORITHM OF DOMINION

It is hard to convince others about the issues you have compromised.

In life the first steps are often the most difficult. First things are often approached with fear and uncertainty. It is true for a child learning to walk and it is true for a new believer learning to walk in the new life of Christ. There are spiritual dynamics involved in learning to live the life of faith.

An algorithm is about processing life. The recent book *Algorithms to Live By*[1] notes that life requires a balance between looking and leaping (Brian Christian and Tom Griffiths, 2016). As noted earlier, Kahneman and Tversky, called it "thinking fast and slow." The term algorithm comes from a ninth century mathematician who wrote about how to solve math problems. The earliest known algorithms, however, are from a four thousand-year-old clay tablet found near Baghdad. It shows the steps for solving long division problems. An algorithm, then, is a series of steps to solve a problem. Algorithms are not just found in mathematics and science. Recipes for baking a cake or your favorite lasagna are algorithms. Algorithms have been part of life since the beginning. Christian and Griffiths say:

> Life is full of problems that are, quite simply, hard. And the mistakes made by people often say more about the intrinsic difficulties [of life] than the fallibility of human brains. (5)

Early in his ministry Pastor Gooding was asked to counsel a marriage. It didn't go well because the couple decided they would just have a fight during the counseling session. Later, when Gooding asked their pastor about the marriage he was told, "I've counseled them. They know what to do, they just won't do it." This is common. Sometimes persons who have made bad decisions say, "I knew it was wrong, but I did it anyway." In other words, we can know what to do, we just don't do it.

The problem is often we leap before we look. Danny Kahneman's *Thinking Fast and Slow* describes it as living by hunches, impressions, past experiences and what everybody else is doing. People often make decisions and established behaviors based on these intangibles rather than on what is actually happening. Jesus met a man at the Pool of Bethesda who complained saying, "I have no one to help me," and "Someone else gets there before me." He could not see any other way to be healed except someone helping him. He could not see how to make a first move unless someone helped him. He had remained in the same way for thirty-eight years. Jesus ignored the excuse and commanded the man to get up and walk. He did. "Take away the gut feeling," Kahneman says, "and judgements improve."

An algorithm, then, is a series of steps used to solve a hard problem (or an easy one). Believers are often clueless about how to make their Christian life work. They are unable to see the steps they must take to have spiritual dominion. As Pastor Marks discovered with the homeless in his city, they have no clue as to what steps they must take in order to get their lives back together following a calamity. The calamity becomes the defining moment of their life. Everything in their life is viewed through the one unsettling event. It is like their life stopped the moment everything was turned upside-down. The defining moment became the lens through which all of life is viewed. In many ways people are often like toddlers learning to walk. Their shifting weight as they move causes them to veer from side to side, never reaching what they set out to obtain. They are literally toddlers. People can be that way too.

Deliverance to Dominion

Dominion often depends on the first step. It is the step that seems impossible, or we fear to take. Hence the complaint, "I have no one to help me." What is heard, much of the time, is the whining sound of someone saying, "I can't." One pastor, recently visiting a church member in the hospital for rehabilitation from a stroke, heard it said repeatedly, "I can't." Well, it really was 'do something or you are going to die!' It is often the first step toward dominion that is the most important and the most difficult.

It is difficult to get past the threshold of inaction and start the process of living in dominion. There is a chemistry to friendships, relationships, marriages, finances, addictions and many other things. In fact, these are what makes society tick. To get the first step to proceed in a chemical reaction, a catalyst or enzyme is needed. A catalyst helps a chemical reaction proceed by lowering the amount of energy needed to begin the first step.

Diabetics are familiar with insulin. Insulin is a hormone that acts as a catalyst. It is produced in the pancreas and secreted into the blood stream. It opens a "gate" in the cell membrane for absorption of glucose (the source of energy for the cells of the body). When there is insufficient insulin (as in Type 1 diabetics) or insulin resistance (as in Type 2 diabetics) then glucose does not enter the cells. In the blood stream it remains unusable. Insulin lowers the energy needed to get glucose (sugar) into your tissues. Insulin is not food. It acts as a key that unlocks the gate for glucose to get where it is needed. Catalysts make the first step of a process possible.

Dominion is made real when certain spiritual activities move God to be involved in your life. Many, if not most, believers have difficulty in seeing the connections between spiritual activities and the dominion they need in life. They say, "I need to make money. What does prayer have to do with that?" Or they say, "I need my rest. What is all the fuss about going to church?"

Many know about the rapture. They do not always know its importance to dominion. The crucial element of worship in dominion is often missed by believers. Many believers do not see the empowering dynamic of fasting and prayer. It is possible that Christians, by and large, do not understand the deceptive nature of the flesh. Spiritual actions are catalysts enabling spiritual dominion in the midst of life's hard things.

In 1972, Mark IV Pictures released *A Thief in the Night*. It was written by Jim Grant and produced by Donald W. Thompson. The 69-minute film is perhaps the most widely distributed Christian film of all time. It is the dramatized story of the events leading up to and following the rapture of the church. It portrays the life of a non-believer, Patty (played by Patty Dunning), whose husband is caught away in the rapture. Patty, however, is left behind. The Gooding's saw the film the first Sunday they attended a recently pioneered Foursquare church, now a Potter's House Christian Fellowship Church. Sunday night they also saw their first "Jesus People" wedding. The wedding party stood up in front of the congregation during the service, the couple repeated the vows, said their "I do's" and all sat down. Then everyone, including the wedding party, watched the movie, *A Thief in the Night*. That was interesting.

After seeing the end time films, Pastor Campbell commented that they did two things in Connie's and his life. First, it moved them to focus on living a righteous lifestyle for God. Second, it motivated them to do something for God. Jesus is coming again.

Many Jesus People of the seventies were moved in the same way. The end time movies brought them over the threshold from knowing a doctrine to doing something for God. The movies were catalysts. They stirred evangelism and a lifestyle beyond just knowing words and "what we believe." The end time movies crystallized the Christian experience as a lifestyle of righteous living and active service for God.

The end times are not just the revealing of Christ. They also expose the anti-Christ. The devil's strategy and aim are revealed in the events of the end times. The anti-Christ is a rival to the throne of God and craves the worship of believers. 2nd Thessalonians says:

> Let no one deceive you by any means; for that Day will not come unless the falling away comes first, and the man of sin is revealed, the son of perdition, 4 who opposes and exalts himself above all that is called God or that is worshiped, so that he sits as God in the temple of God, showing himself that he is God. (2 Thessalonians 2:3-4)

Worship is an issue the demonic personality Satan is willing to do battle over. His desire is to sit on the throne of God as God. Worship in spirit and truth (John 4:23-24) belongs to only the one true God. In praise and worship God is enthroned. In Revelation 13 two beasts arise at the end. One is from the sea. It is given forty-two weeks to overcome the saints of God. All whose names are not written in the Lamb's Book of Life will worship this beast. The other beast arises from the earth. This second beast is given power to deceive those who dwell on the earth and to make an image that is empowered with breath and speech. This beast causes all who will not worship the demonic image to be killed. This beast also causes all to be marked in order to buy or sell. Without the mark (of the beast) they cannot participate in the last days economy.

> He was granted power to give breath to the image of the beast, that the image of the beast should both speak and cause as many as would not worship the image of the beast to be killed. (Revelation 13:15)

Worship is critical. It is a must. It is an issue of life and death. Worship is a vital step toward dominion.

The dramatic battle for worship is graphically displayed in the events of Daniel. The three Hebrew children, captive in Babylon, gain favor within the empire. But their refusal to bow down to the giant gold image of Nebuchadnezzar set up in the plain of Dura is a crime punishable by death. Many would recognize the story of the fiery furnace. It was heated seven times hotter than normal. The three Hebrew slaves refused to worship Nebuchadnezzar's image. The rage and fury of his demonically driven nature changed his countenance. The three Hebrews responded to Nebuchadnezzar's fury but remained unmoved to worship an image.

> Shadrach, Meshach, and Abed-Nego answered and said to the king, "O Nebuchadnezzar, we have no need to answer you in this matter. 17 If that is the case, our God whom we serve is able to deliver us from the burning fiery furnace, and He will deliver us from your hand, O king. 18 But if not, let it be known to you, O king, that we do not serve your gods, nor will we worship the gold image which you have set up." (Daniel 3:16-18)

They did not bow down. They were bound and thrown into the fiery furnace. In a great demonstration and testimony of God's power to deliver, they survived the fiery furnace. Then, the astonished Nebuchadnezzar made a decree:

> "Blessed be the God of Shadrach, Meshach, and Abed-Nego, who sent His Angel and delivered His servants who trusted in Him, and they have frustrated the king's word, and yielded their bodies, that they should not serve nor worship any god except their own God! 29 Therefore I make a decree that any people, nation, or language which speaks anything amiss against the God of Shadrach, Meshach, and Abed-Nego shall be cut in pieces, and their houses shall be made an ash heap; because there is no other God who can deliver like this. 30 Then the king promoted Shadrach, Meshach, and Abed-Nego in the province of Babylon." (Daniel 3:28-29)

True worship was a catalyst to empowerment and testimony for the three Hebrews. One cannot be too busy to worship.

Islamic worship dominates much of the Arab world. Buddhist worship dominates much of the Oriental world. Traditional or Indigenous worship dominates many third world nations. In Jesus day Judaism dominated Jerusalem and Israel. When Lucifer was cast out of heaven the scripture notes that he "weakened" the nations. Nations are weakened when they worship false gods. National issues are often established based on the cultural "religion." As Bob Dillon noted in the song, "You Gotta Serve Somebody."[2]

> You may be the heavyweight champion of the world.
> You may be a socialite with a long string of pearls.
> But you're gonna have to serve somebody, yes
> Indeed you're gonna have to serve somebody
> Well, it may be the devil or it may be the Lord
> But you're gonna have to serve somebody.

In Jesus third temptation in the wilderness (Matthew 4:8-10), the devil offers the power, wealth and influence of the nations in exchange for worship. The demonic world has a lustful craving for worship. It craves the worship that belongs only to God. It is interesting to note in church services that the lukewarm soul, the backslider and the carnally minded will not get involved in worship. The difference maker in one's life is often the step to be a worshipper. People are worshippers by nature.

Luke tells of the woman who came and worshipped at Jesus feet.

> Then one of the Pharisees asked Him to eat with him. And He went to the Pharisee's house, and sat down to eat. 37 And behold, a woman in the city who was a sinner, when she knew that Jesus sat at the table in the Pharisee's house, brought an alabaster flask of fragrant oil, 38 and stood at His feet behind Him weeping; and she began to wash His feet with her tears, and wiped them with the hair of her head; and she kissed His feet and anointed them with the fragrant oil. (Luke 7:36-38)

Her worship provoked a controversy. True worship often does (John 12:4-6). The host, a Pharisee, thought to himself that Jesus must not be a true prophet. Jesus received worship from a sinner. Jesus confronted Simon with a riddle. Who would love more, Jesus queried, "A person forgiven little or a person forgiven much?" Of course, the one forgiven much was the Pharisee's reply.

> [Jesus] turned to the woman and said to Simon [the Pharisee] "Do you see this woman? I entered your house; you gave Me no water for My feet, but she has washed My feet with her tears and wiped them with the hair of her head. 45 You gave Me no kiss, but this woman has not ceased to kiss My feet since the time I came in. 46 You did not anoint My head with oil, but this woman has anointed My feet with fragrant oil. 47 Therefore I say to you, her sins, which

are many, are forgiven, for she loved much. But to whom little is forgiven, the same loves little." (Luke 7:44-47)

Then [Jesus] said to her, "Your sins are forgiven." (Luke 7:48)

The implication is Simon and the others criticize worship, because they do not love "much."

Jesus ends the third temptation saying, "Away with you, Satan! For it is written, 'You shall worship the Lord your God, and Him only you shall serve.'" That's the issue. Who do you serve? Who do you love? Who is glorified in your life? Those who are undefiled by the world refuse to worship the devil. The undefiled worship with a new song (Revelation 14:3). Those who worship the beast have no rest day or night. The smoke of their torment ascends forever and ever. The throne of heaven opens to worship with lifted hands, lifted voices and lifted hearts. Worship leads to dominion over the cares of the world.

Worship and a view to eternity, are two spiritual dynamics of dominion. They are often the difference between living in dominion and falling in the wilderness. Another spiritual dynamic that leads to dominion involves the flesh.

Flesh dwells with you and in you. The Greek word is *sarx*. It is used in a wide variety of New Testament contexts. It describes both raw meat and an inner quality of human life. In the context of dominion, it refers to a "latent power of the soul," (Watchman Nee's phrase).[3] It lurks within a person. Flesh describes a person whose life is carnal (fleshly) and focused on the things of the world (Romans 8:5). Flesh enflames passions for fulfilling the lusts of the children of wrath (Ephesians 2:2-3). It is the latent power of the old life of sin and corruption.

Flesh is self. Paul writes, "But now, it is no longer I who do it, but sin that dwells in me. For I know that in me (that is, in my flesh) nothing good dwells; for to will is present with me, but how to perform what is good I do not find (Romans 7:17-18)." And Jeremiah says, "Cursed is the man who trusts in man, / And makes flesh his strength (Romans 17:5)." Flesh is about what you feel and what you want. Flesh hates sacrifice and correction. Flesh does not like being told, "No." Flesh is the bridge from the demonic world outside to one's inner world of the soul, heart and mind. Flesh cannot please God (Romans 8:8). Flesh is at war with the Spirit and pushes one's life toward what one hates (Galatians 5:17).

Flesh must be cut away. Circumcision is about cutting away and casting flesh aside. Paul says everyone in Israel who claims to be a Jew is not really a Jew. Paul draws an analogy from cutting away the flesh in physical circumcision to the (fleshy) nature of the heart.

> For he is not a Jew who is one outwardly, nor is circumcision that which is outward in the flesh; 29 but he is a Jew who is one inwardly; and circumcision [cutting away flesh] is that of the heart, in the Spirit, not in the letter; whose praise is not from men but from God. (Romans 2:28-29)

The latent power of the soul taps the issues of our carnal nature and sense of time. It is deceptive because flesh is not always seen as a "right now" issue. It is not seen as something to be dealt with immediately. We view it as something to be dealt with later. Because it is not a "right now" issue, our flesh or carnal nature is spared from being brought under control. It is allowed to lie latent and undealt with spiritually. It is likely we will be amazed at what gave us trouble spiritually. Much of our trouble was really un-dealt-with flesh. Often flesh goes unnoticed until it manifests. Then it creates conflict with people and the Spirit of God.

It is hard for God to convict you of the issues you have compromised. Abraham's nephew, Lot, compromised when he chose life in the well-watered plain of the Jordan River. He settled his family and made his life in Sodom. He became one of its prominent citizens. Lot, however, was in danger when God chose to destroy the wicked city. At the urging of his angelic visitors, Lot began to flee but was unable to convince his family to leave. Even Lot's wife looked back on the life she was leaving and was turned into a pillar of salt. Interestingly, Lot never returned to Abraham or the household he came from. It is hard to return to what you have compromised. It is hard to convince others about things you have personally compromised.

Compromise is an action of the flesh. The flesh weakens human nature. It is not transformed. It must be cut away. It is decayed, corrupted and sinful. The flesh is what you become because of sin. It is self, the self-nature and the target of hell. It is what is lurking within you. It is not God or godly. It is not the voice of God.

The voice of the flesh, if you listen carefully, sounds very much like your voice. You are hearing what the flesh desires and wants. Flesh wants to spare itself from sacrifice and denial. It cries out that it can be dealt with later. The voice of the flesh—its language—is not the language of love, service and labor. It is not the language of sacrifice and pain. It is the language of compromise and pleasing self. It is the language of carnality. It is unlikely you'll ever be tempted in a language you do not know. Temptation is in the language you speak.

Ponder the life of Samson. He was birthed and empowered to deliver Israel from the Philistines. His destiny was to be a deliverer from the Philistine's oppression of Israel. Samson, however, took a Philistine wife. Samson caroused with Philistine harlots. Delilah, his temptress, was a Philistine. It's hard to impress others with your God when you are compromised. Samson could not deliver Israel from the people he chose to dwell among.

It is hard to judge the culture you've chosen to live in. It's hard to judge the old friends and soul mates when you still want to live among them. It is very hard to stand against and judge your own cultural flesh and blood. It is one of the problems missionaries must deal with. It is hard for converts to renounce the sin and ungodliness of their indigenous culture. Many things indigenous people claim as culture is not "culture." It is sin or idolatry. It was not until his dying moments that Samson brought any deliverance to Israel. Never during his life did he deliver Israel from the oppression of the Philistines. Samson saw a woman and said to his father, "Get her for me," because, "She pleases me." It's the language and voice of the flesh. It comes from within.

This is made painfully clear to Moses. Moses met and was commissioned by God at the burning bush. Moses was to deliver the nation of Israel from bondage in Egypt. It was his calling. He left Midian with his wife and two sons. On the way, God arrested him and sought to kill him. This is astounding. God is willing to kill his chosen deliverer. What was the issue? Moses had not circumcised his two sons. His wife, Zipporah, took a sharp stone and circumcised the boys casting the bloody flesh at the feet of Moses. She said, "Surely you are a husband of blood to me (Exodus 4:24-26)!" And God let Moses go.

Moses was willing to compromise his family by sparing them from sacrifice. Zipporah did what Moses was unwilling to do. Compromise plays out in the home. Moses lost dominion in his home, even though he was the chosen and commissioned leader and deliverer of the nation.

Compromise for the sake of the flesh is throughout the Bible. Two more poignant—keenly sad—examples will suffice. The "blessing" of sons by their father is an important event in Hebrew and many other cultures. When it came time for Jacob to bless his sons, the keenest and saddest words were to his firstborn, Rueben.

> Reuben, you are my firstborn, / My might and the beginning of my strength, / The excellency of dignity and the excellency of power. / 4 Unstable as water, you shall not excel, / Because you went up to your father's bed [Genesis 35:22]; / Then you defiled it—He went up to my couch. (Genesis 49:3-4)

The occasion Jacob is referring to is Rueben's affair with Bilhah, one of Jacob's concubines. Jacob also did not spare Levi and Simeon of whom he says:

> In their anger they slew a man, And in their self-will they hamstrung an ox. 7 Cursed be their anger, for it is fierce; And their wrath, for it is cruel! I will divide them in Jacob And scatter them in Israel (Genesis 49:6-7).

Again, Jacob reaches back to an earlier time. Simeon and Levi conspired against their father's will to kill the man who violated their sister, Dinah (Genesis 34). In their flesh (self-will) they conspired.

The second poignant occasion is David's refusal to judge his sons (e.g. Absalom, 2 Samuel 13) and his own flesh (e.g. the affair with Bathsheba, 2 Samuel 11). David lost dominion at home. Failure to deal with the flesh cost him. His son died. Rebellion rose in his own household. He had a good man murdered. These were tragic marks on David's résumé as king.

The flesh you spare today is the flesh that will destroy you tomorrow. The deception of thinking time is on your side is common, but it is not true. Compromise has a long reach. Reuben's family never produced a single leader. David's family was filled with bloody conflict. Saul spared King Agag's life (flesh) even though he was clearly told to not spare it. It cost him his kingdom. Ministry is purchased at the cost of your flesh. It is purchased at the cost of your self-will, self-desire and your *want-to*.

People say, "But this is what I *want-to* do." Jesus tells the disciples who were unable to cast out the demon that afflicted a young boy, "This kind does not go out except by prayer and fasting (Matthew 17:21)." This kind of ministry—deliverance and healing—requires the sacrifice of the flesh.

Time is no friend to the flesh. The movie starlets of yesterday are not what they used to be. The old flame or heart-throb you want to look up on the internet or fantasize about is not the same. Look at the word— old! The flesh changes with time. Compromise for the sake of the flesh will not preserve it. It is passing away. It doesn't matter how much money you invest in collagen and Botox, time is no friend to the flesh.

Dominion is impossible unless one steps into the spiritual dynamics. It is important to see life in terms of eternity. Worship is a powerful dynamic in establishing a favorable relationship with God. Compromise for the sake of the flesh will cost you dominion. There is, perhaps no greater hindrance, however, than the lack of prayer and fasting. The absence of the simple tools of dominion—prayer, fasting and biblical literacy account for the extraordinary shallowness of modern Christianity. The Christian experience of many who claim the name of Christ is only skin deep. Scratch them with a problem and they are ready to backslide and cry to the world about their painful experience with Christianity.

People in crisis often fail to apply God's most powerful weapons—prayer and fasting. This is probably because these weapons place a demand on the flesh. Campbell tells the story of his father's 32-inch, full-choke, 12-gauge shotgun. It was for hunting squirrels. It worked. However, it had a tremendous kick. Pastor Campbell liked to say it killed at both ends. His friend had a new 12-gauge shotgun that was more comfortable to use but not as effective. Fasting and prayer, Campbell commonly says, also kills at both ends. It kills the demonic and the flesh.

In Mark 9:29 Jesus made the statement: "This kind can come out by nothing but prayer and fasting." Clearly, there are some issues that require prayer and fasting. Jesus made the statement to a faithless generation. It was a generation that had no faith in the tools God provides for spiritual battle. Earlier in the story Jesus says, "If you can believe, all things are possible to him who believes (Mark 9:23)." At the core of the story is an "unclean" spirit that took hold of a young boy and tried to kill him. Jesus delivered the boy from the unclean spirit. The disciples tried to deliver the boy, but they could not. In response to their ineffective efforts they asked Jesus why? Jesus responded with the statement about fasting and prayer.

In the spiritual arena, fasting gives weight or "k-thud" to prayer. It makes prayer effective. It moves God. It energizes faith. Fasting is far more than not eating. People in great distress or grief are often unable to eat. They may be going through a divorce, the death of a loved one or depression. Fasting to afflict the soul, however, must be accompanied by prayer. Fasting is an outward expression of what is happening in the inner man. It is an agony and passion of the soul to move God on behalf of human need.

The Prophet Joel tells a backslidden nation to "lament" as a "virgin in sackcloth" (Joel 1:8, 13). The picture is that of a young woman wearing a black goats-hair cloth that chafes against her skin. Perhaps as one who is in mourning over the loss of a loved one. Joel calls three classes of people to lament. The elders, the drunkards, and the priests are to see their true backslidden spiritual condition and lament. An agricultural disaster had destroyed the crops and vineyards of the land. The grain, wine and oil had been devoured by pestilence. Their entire society is unable to function because they could not carry out their religious obligations and sacrifices. Originally, *lament,* meant to pull out the hair and beard and to beat one's chest. It came to mean to wail as a mourner. Joel calls on the nation to lament or act like one who mourns the death of a loved one. God is calling for action.

> "Now, therefore," says the Lord, "Turn to Me with all your heart, With fasting, with weeping, and with mourning." 13 So rend your heart, and not your garments; Return to the Lord your God, For He is gracious and merciful, Slow to anger, and of great kindness; And He relents from doing harm. (Joel 2:12-13)

God asks for a rending of the heart. It is like wringing out wet clothes. In disaster God says, show me your heart if you want me to move. Fasting kills at both ends. It detox's the flesh and neutralizes the demonic.

Prayer links one to God's purposes. Jesus prayer in the Garden of Gethsemane was over the will of God. Elijah had human passions as we do. He prayed and was linked to the purposes of God.

> Elijah was a man with a nature like ours, and he prayed earnestly that it would not rain; and it did not rain on the land for three years and six months. 18 And he prayed again, and the heaven gave rain, and the earth produced its fruit. (James 5:17-18)

Prayer locks one in step with God. Prayer establishes boundaries and cements decisions in place. Prayer and fasting move one beyond the intellect and rationalism of the modern world. It moves one past soulish emotionalism.

The absence of prayer and fasting is the reason for the great shallowness in modern Christianity. It is the reason Christians lack spiritual understanding and are ineffective in their testimony. Daniel says:

> I, Daniel, understood by the books (Daniel 9:2) ... Then I set my face toward the Lord God (Daniel 9:3)

Prayer for Daniel was not a laundry list of wants and supposed needs. It was set in the solid understanding of the Word of God. How will you know how to pray if you don't know the will of God? Daniel understood God's plan by reading Jeremiah's prophetic word. Daniel set his face toward God and prayed for the reality of God's promise to national Israel.

Sometimes it is hard to grasp the importance of prayer. Daniel's prayer transforms his understanding of God. It becomes more than doctrine and theology. It becomes more than a calculus or balance sheet of right and wrong. In crises we often learn more about God because he is much more than we assume. The question—how long—is a question that has come into the heart of Daniel. He is asking, "What is the Future of Israel?"

It is the same question Paul asks in Romans 9-11.

What about *my* future? Good question, isn't it?

"You'll never change the world if the world has changed you." Sin has never been subtler or more pervasive than it is today. The demonic does not surrender to a saint soiled by the world of sin. The demonic judges spiritual authority by the dominion one has over the flesh. If you can refuse food, then you can probably refuse anything.

Fasting and prayer drag the flesh into submission. Fasting and prayer accomplish something in the area of your greatest enemy—the flesh. As with the flesh, the lack of prayer and fasting does not appear significant until you are in a crisis. It doesn't seem significant until you must exercise authority for deliverance. Paul's comment is, "In my flesh dwells no good thing (Romans 7:18)." Paul did not find his flesh doing what he desired. It must be overcome. Your tolerance for sin sets the boundaries on your prayers. The sin you excuse, the sin you tolerate, and the sin you serve will bite and devour you in the end.

Prayer and fasting "chasten" the soul (Psalm 69:10). They are not popular in the world. The world accepts ritual prayer and prayer for appearances. Real prayer drags the flesh into submission. It is a different matter and the world mocks as a dog barks at a stranger. They mocked Jesus. They laughed him to scorn when he said, "The girl is not dead (Luke 8:52)." The covetous Pharisees derided (openly sneered) him (Luke 16:14). If you traffic in the things of the world, you'll become as polluted as the world and be powerless over the fleshly nature.

The steps, the algorithm, for dominion are not hard. Faith includes something you believe, something you say, and something you do. The spiritual dynamics for dominion in life are not theories. They are actions done in faith. Living in righteousness, laboring for the kingdom of God, worshipping in spirit and truth, cutting away the flesh, prayer and fasting—These are the spiritual dynamics for dominion.

CHAPTER 8

BORN FOR DOMINION

Rights without duty is like breathing with one lung. Solzhenitsyn

Deliverance is when God comes down. It is external, from above and not within human nature. We cannot make heaven or find our way through life on our own. God must come down to us in power and grace. Deliverance is real, powerful, meaningful and important. It must become active in life. It must become dominion. When deliverance is activated by faith it becomes powerful in punishing all disobedience and casting down the strongholds of the demonic. That's dominion.

God's design was for man (men and women), "created in his image (Genesis 1:28-29)," to have dominion over all of creation. God established this at the creation.

> So God created man in His own image; in the image of God He created him; male and female He created them. 28 Then God blessed them, and God said to them, "Be fruitful and multiply; fill the earth and subdue it; have dominion over the fish of the sea, over the birds of the air, and over every living thing that moves on the earth. (Genesis 1:28-29)

In the New Testament Jesus noted this dominion also established rule and power over the spiritual principalities and powers of darkness. We have a right as believers in Christ to be free from demonic oppression.

> Behold, I give you the authority to trample on serpents and scorpions, and over all the power of the enemy, and nothing shall by any means hurt you. 20 Nevertheless do not rejoice in this, that the spirits are subject to you, but rather rejoice because your names are written in heaven." (Luke 10:19)

In every human, God has deposited his own likeness and given the right to rule as a sovereign. While disputing with the Pharisees, Jesus said in John 10,

> Is it not written in your law, "I said, 'You are gods?'" (John 10:34)

The word gods, in this case, simply means sovereigns. You have the right to rule in your own life. Of course, it does not mean you will be the boss in every endeavor. It does not mean you are perfection. It does not mean you replace God. Obviously, we see the evidence of sin's corruption on every hand. Deliverance restores the right to dominion in life. The question is, "Are you living in dominion?" We are not talking about dominance. Have you cast down, pulled down, brought into captivity, and punished every wrong way of thinking and activity? Have you come to know God's dominion?

After ministering and teaching along the lakeshore in Galilee, Jesus was alone with his disciples. He said, "Let's cross to the other side of the lake (Mark 4:35)." During the crossing a fierce storm threatened to sink the boat. Jesus, asleep in the back of the boat, was awakened. He calmed the storm with a rebuke, "Silence! Be still!" After crossing, they entered the region of Decapolis. It was a Greco-Roman league of ten cities. All but one of which were across the lake and opposite Galilee. It included the area of Gadara. Jesus arrival marked a visit to an area shunned by Jews. It was a non-Jewish desert region that had been ruled by Persia. It was a pagan culture. Some say it may have been the Prodigal Son's destination when he left home. As in other Greek dominated cultures they worshipped the human body, exalted nakedness and desired a life of wealth and luxury. It was a region filled from antiquity with Baal worship, perversion and child sacrifice.

When they arrived and set foot on shore Jesus was met by a man possessed by a spirit. He lived in a burial cave among the tombs. He wandered about howling and cutting himself. When he saw Jesus arrive, he ran to meet him and bowed down before him. Jesus commanded the evil spirit to leave the man, but the demonic personality begged to be left alone.

> With a shriek, he screamed, "Why are you interfering with me, Jesus, Son of the Most High God? In the name of God, I beg you, don't torture me!" 8 For Jesus had already said to the spirit, "Come out of the man, you evil spirit." (Mark 5:7-8 NLT)

This "Gadarene's" sin had taken him beyond his and his parents plans for his life. We don't know what his mother thought when she was held in her arms for the first time. We don't know what hope she had for his future. His father might have seen a future in him that assumed a family business or profession. His father might have desired for him to become a craftsman or even a statesman. But his world was turned upside down. Maybe it was genetic or an inherited disease that caused the insanity. It could have been an accident in childhood that opened the door to the demonic possession. Maybe it was simply the downward spiral in sinfulness. Whatever the past may have been, this man was possessed by a legion of spiritual entities — some estimates are as many as six thousand. These demonic powers inspired and controlled him. Demon possession is pictured in the Bible as this kind of unrestrained behavior. The demonic had gained access and then dominion over this man's life. It was not the life anyone thought he was born to live.

While Campbell was pastoring in Illinois there was a young man who was always in trouble. He had a violent relationship with his mother. He was disobedient and physically aggressive. One day his mother disappeared. The young man was found, arrested, charged and convicted of her murder. His father was a good man who had wealth and influence but did not have dominion in his home. The demonic elements had gained a stronghold in his son's life. The father pleaded with Pastor Campbell to help his son. He pleaded for help for himself. His son's anger, his aggression, and continued involvement in the demonic and occult world took him beyond what he thought possible. He did what he had not dreamed of doing. He eventually died in prison.

Deliverance is real. Jesus can deliver even in these "impossible" or "institutionalized" cases. Deliverance comes by the Blood of Jesus and in the Name of Jesus. Divine wholeness comes by the blood of Jesus' stripes. Divine power (authority) comes in the Name of Jesus. There is power in the Name of Jesus to break the chains of bondage. The chains of Leviathan's bondage can be more real than the chains they used to bind the Gadarene. The power to heal and deliver, the power to bind and loose—the power of God—is available but must be activated in faith.

Jesus encapsulated his ministry in Nazareth at the beginning of his Galilean ministry (Mark 1-4). He received the scroll of Isaiah in the synagogue and read it. Jesus said the words of Isaiah 61:1-2 applied to himself.

> The Spirit of the Lord is upon me, / for he has anointed me to bring Good News to the poor. / He has sent me to proclaim that captives will be released, / that the blind will see, / that the oppressed will be set free, / and that the time of the Lord's favor has come."
> (Luke 4:18-19 NLT)

Jesus commanded the Gadarene's demonic (unclean) personalities to leave. Jesus questioned them and asked their name. "Legion," was the reply ("My name is Mob. I'm a rioting mob" *MSG*). They implored him not to cast them out or torment them before their time. They pleaded to be sent into the swine. Jesus granted their wish. The swine ran down into the lake and were destroyed. Those who watched it marveled. And they marveled that the man remained, "sitting and clothed and in his right mind." And they were afraid (Mark 5:15).

The demonic personalities know their time is limited. They know they are occupying persons not their own. They understand they can be cast out when people decide and say, "That's enough!" The demonic personalities of perversion and pornography, drugs and alcohol, anger and violence, and depression and self-pity, can be told "enough." The portion or inheritance of the born-again believer is freedom. God is a deliverer. Jesus said it in John,

> "Most assuredly, I say to you, whoever commits sin is a slave of sin. And a slave does not abide in the house forever, but a son abides forever. Therefore if the Son makes you free, you shall be free indeed. (John 8:34-36)

The demons do not want to be sent to hell or scattered. Jesus encourages the redeemed to live a new way that gives no place to the devil in mind or spirit. Paul writes to this issue in Ephesians.

> This I say, therefore, and testify in the Lord, that you should no longer walk as the rest of the Gentiles walk, in the futility of their mind, 18 having their understanding darkened, being alienated from the life of God, because of the ignorance that is in them, because of the blindness of their heart; 19 who, being past feeling, have given themselves over to lewdness, to work all uncleanness with greediness. 20 But you have not so learned Christ, 21 if indeed you have heard Him and have been taught by Him, as the truth is in Jesus: 22 that you put off, concerning your former conduct, the old man which grows corrupt according to the deceitful lusts, 23 and be renewed in the spirit of your mind, 24 and that you put on the new man which was created according to God, in true righteousness and holiness. 25 Therefore, putting away lying, "Let each one of you speak truth with his neighbor," for we are members of one another. 26 "Be angry, and do not sin": do not let the sun go down on your wrath, 27 nor give place to the devil. (Ephesians 4:17-27)

It is shocking how many things are spiritual and how many things operate in the demonic realm. This demon-possessed man was delivered by a command from Jesus. Eugene Peterson's *Message* translation puts it bluntly. Jesus just commanded the tormenting evil spirit saying, "Out! Get out of the man!" (Mark 5:8 *MSG*). This deliverance was executed by words! It was spoken words issued in the authority of Jesus. Jesus had more in mind for this man than just deliverance.

Deliverance must be lived out in the events of life. How you think becomes crucial to your life after deliverance. What are the mental processes when you find yourself in conflict, crisis, or barrenness? How does dominion come into your life?

Achievement and purpose are related to dominion. Campbell, in 1968 knew there had to be more to life than what he was experiencing. He had come home from broken relationships and trouble. His mother asked him, "Son, what's the matter? He replied, "There has to be more to life than this." In February of 1971 he was born again. He said, "I knew then that God had a purpose and cause for my life." Let's ask ourselves, "Are we settling for less than what God would provide?" Jesus called some fishermen to follow him and become fishers of men. That's not much different from the questions Steve Jobs asked successful businessmen. Jobs was asking them, "Do you want to change the world?" Can Jesus call you to leave and follow him? Can Jesus ask, do you want to change the world? Abraham was called and went by faith not knowing the great destiny unfolding through his life and posterity. Can God enlarge your vision? Can God enlarge your destiny? Campbell's prayer became, "God, I want to contribute."

Dominion is established when you "go out" by the will of God. The old phrase is, "Nothing ventured, nothing gained." The demonic personalities of hell will steal your entire life if you allow it. They will keep you from prayer and fasting. They will keep you from conversations with God leading to accomplishment and satisfaction. Jesus says clearly, "The thief does not come except to steal, and to kill, and to destroy. I have come that they may have life, and that they may have it more abundantly (John 10:10)." Peter says, "Be sober, be vigilant; because your adversary the devil walks about like a roaring lion, seeking whom he may devour (1 Peter 5:8)."

When life means nothing, then things become everything. When life is empty things become paramount. God told Abraham to look into the heavens. Is it possible to count the number of stars? God was asking Abraham to consider the possibilities that are in God's power. God hung the heavens on nothing. God can do anything. Abraham and Sarah were barren, but God used them to create a nation. God can do anything.

Anything God says he can do; he is able to do. We have no clue what is possible for God to do in our lives.

> "God is not a man, that He should lie, Nor a son of man, that He should repent. Has He said, and will He not do? Or has He spoken, and will He not make it good? (Number 23:19)

Abraham was told to look into the heavens and consider the greatness and power of God. God created it all by his word. "For since the creation of the world His invisible attributes are clearly seen, being understood by the things that are made, even His eternal power and Godhead (Romans 1:20)." The possibilities offered to Abraham were endless. The same is true for every believer who goes out in faith. Campbell and Gooding marvel at what God has done. It is a marvel to see people with no high school education, former drug addicts, people from fatherless homes and abusive circumstances pastoring large churches and making impact in other nations. Most of these people have no formal theological training, yet they rightly divide the Word of God as they preach the gospel.

The familiar story of Steve Jobs' hiring the successful Pepsi executive, John Sculley, gives insight to what decisions are about:

> "Do you want to sell sugar water for the rest of your life, or do you want to come with me and change the world?"[1]

Steve Jobs asked John Sculley the question. It is part of the reason Sculley joined Apple. Jobs advocates using life to make a "dent" in the world. One's life should count on the world's stage.

The other commonly told Steve Jobs story is about a VP hire. He interviewed one of IBM's successful executive officers, Stephen Sonnenfeld.

> [Steve] Job's response when Sonnenfeld told him what he did was, "Anyone can throw money at things, what are they doing that's really good for the world?" Sonnenfeld maintained he was already doing

well and Jobs ended the interview saying, "Yeah I have a problem with the work, but that's not what really concerns me. What I can't accept is that you were able to do this for many years and still get up in the morning and look at yourself in the mirror."

The problem in this generation is often that we are taught to fail. The term we frequently see is "boomerang children." It's children who may leave home for marriage, college, job or something they desire but within a short time they are back home and living on their parent's income. One judge ordered a man to move out of his parent's home. He was thirty years old and complained that for eight years he had never had to do that. Forty-two percent of millennial's chose socialism. It seems they must imagine it means free money, free food, and a free ride. It must be a life without effort, cost or discipline. However, you cannot turn your life over to the government or anyone else without surrendering your dominion. You must surrender your right to rule when you give the demonic access to your mind.

A cartoon showed a kid hoisting a trophy and saying, "I didn't have to do anything." The next frame showed the child, now elderly, lifting up a check and saying, "I got a check and didn't have to work." When you ponder the sentiment of a generation that wants rewards without earning or effort, it is easy to see why there is no dominion.

A schoolgirl tried out for cheerleader at Hanover Park High School. Her mother complained when she was cut from the squad. She didn't make the team. She and her mother threw such a fit that the athletic director changed the team's policy so the wannabe cheerleader could be on the team. Think about that. The other girls did think about it. They brought a grievance to the school board. One sophomore said, "I did not put in 18 months of work to lead up to this moment just to be told it didn't matter anymore." Another student said, "I tried my hardest. Now everything is going away because of one child ... all my hard work is thrown out the window." Once they thought about it, they understood that their efforts, training and performance were actually being disqualified. They understood their efforts and training actually did not matter.

Lowering standards has become an epidemic. It happened to the New York Fire Department when a female applicant could not meet the requirements. She was given an $81,000/year desk job. The same can be seen in military combat training. Jessica Lahey comments in her best selling book, *The Gift of Failure*, "Kids are smarter than we give them credit for, and they know when we lower our expectations for them.... They no longer trust us to be honest and unbiased."[2]

Esau is the Old Testament model of unthinking surrender to the appetites of the world. Later, when the consequences became clear, he became bitter. It was his choice. His bitterness defiled the whole family.

> Looking carefully lest anyone fall short of the grace of God; lest any root of bitterness springing up cause trouble, and by this many become defiled; ... or profane ... like Esau, who for one morsel of food sold his birthright. 17 For you know that afterward, when he wanted to inherit the blessing, he was rejected, for he found no place for repentance, though he sought it diligently with tears.
> (Hebrews 12:15-17)

Dominion is not automatic. It must be sought and personally possessed. We can admire sports figures that have great achievements. We can admire athletes that can make the jump shot like LeBron James or Michael Jordan. But it didn't just happen for them. It took work. It took thousands of hours of concentrated work. It was more than "natural ability." Angela Duckworth's personal story and her book (*Grit: the Power of Passion and Perseverance*, Scribner, 2018) tell the tale admirably. Michael Jordan said, "Maybe I made it look too easy."

God has made believers to be more than conquerors. Today the trend is to rename everything to make it sound like we are accomplishing something. When you say crawling is "walking," you are still not walking. You are only deceiving yourself. Abraham Lincoln is reported to have asked, "How many legs does a sheep have if you call its tail a leg?" Sheep have four legs no matter what you call its tail. It has been said that all Royalty must learn to ski. That is so they can learn how to fall. C. S. Lewis has commented that pain is a great teacher.

The believer must pull down, cast down and bring every thought into captivity and punish every thought that opposes God and godliness. False thoughts and imaginations must be "punished" to the point they are incapacitated. They must be locked up so they can cause no harm. Dominion is a personal responsibility. Each one must own what is right personally. You must own your own words, feelings, emotions, desires and vision.

It is interesting when you think of Peter. He was the leader of the apostolic band of twelve. He came to a place where he thought he had dominion. He thought he would never forsake or deny Jesus. If you go to Israel you can stand in the courtyard of Caiaphas, the high priest's house. You can see the statues commemorating Peter's denial of Jesus. He denied, not once, but three times. Then, hearing the rooster crow, he wept bitterly. He did not possess the dominion he thought he did.

Jesus healed a woman who had been bent over for eighteen years. She was a Jew, one of God's children. When a controversy erupted about healing on the Sabbath, Jesus said, "Ought not this woman, being a daughter of Abraham, whom Satan has bound—think of it—for eighteen years, be loosed from this bond (Luke 13:16)?" Dominion belongs to the children of God. Matthew writes of the desperate woman from Canaan whose daughter was severely demon-possessed. She pleaded for her daughter's healing. Jesus bluntly told her, "It is not good to take the children's bread and throw it to the little dogs (Matthew 15:26)." In other words, healing is for the children of God. Healing is the children's bread. The woman persisted and noted that dogs eat of the crumbs from the children's table. Jesus marveled at her and said, "O woman, great is your faith! Let it be to you as you desire (Matthew 15:28)." The woman had taken dominion in her own life and pleaded for her daughter. She had to cast down what her neighbors said, what the doctors might have said, what her culture said, and what her own fears said. She had to turn to Jesus in faith. She had to believe Jesus was who said he was, the Son of God. Jesus marveled at her faith.

In 1987 the Campbells went to pioneer a church in Malaysia. It was a nation in chaos when they arrived. *The New York Times* ran the headline on October 30, 1987, "Wave of Opposition Arrests: 3 Days That Shook Malaysia." The article went on to say:

> Malaysians tell stories of the last 72 hours with expressions of disbelief.
>
> A social critic disabled by polio was seized by more than half a dozen policemen; five environmentalist were imprisoned as national security risks ... the leader of the opposition in Parliament was detained ... without charges or the right to a hearing.[3]

In all, 81 politicians and civic leaders were detained, and four newspapers were suspended. The Campbells had to leave the country and return when things calmed down. It was a difficult time. It was especially difficult on Connie. There wasn't anything she liked about Malaysia. She didn't like the food. She didn't like driving on the left side of the road. She didn't like the climate, the city or the culture. She wanted to leave and go home.

After arguing and hashing out the issues of people who depended on them and costs already expended, to no satisfactory conclusion, Pastor Campbell said to Connie, "I'm going to call Pastor Mitchell." That is, he was going to call his headship and leader of their Fellowship of Churches. Connie said, "Go ahead." So, Campbell called and explained to his pastor what was happening. He explained that Connie wanted to leave and go back home. Connie was nearby and listening during the call. There was no speakerphone or extension at that time. Pastor Mitchell said, "Tell Connie she can't come home." So, Campbell turned to Connie and said, "Pastor Mitchell says you can't go home." Connie responded, "OK."

The issue was settled. They stayed. To this day Connie loves Malaysia. The food, the people and the city are all things that excite her when they travel back to Malaysia. They continue to oversee a thriving ministry in Malaysia.

One of the things often missed in dominion is the factor of leadership. There is a powerful dimension that comes when your life is lived in submission to leadership. Biblically, the present world and the heavenly run in parallel. When the Gooding's were first married, they attended the Eagle Rock Christian Assembly (a Foursquare church in a district of Los Angeles). The pastor had been a long-term teacher at the Foursquare Bible School. He taught, among other things, Greek and Hebrew. At the time the Gooding's attended he was teaching about—and it went on for weeks—the kingdom of God. "It is," he said, "A Federal Headship." The kingdom of God has, in other words, a headship or leadership structure. It is the structure established by God. It is not ruled by a committee of men.

Understanding submission and authority, he said, are crucial to understanding God and how the kingdom of God works. It is also crucial to understanding how salvation works. Understanding these things became crucial to the Gooding's future. When they moved to Sierra Vista, Arizona in 1976, they had plans and ideas about ministry and their future. Submission to leadership, however, gave them key spiritual direction critical for their future.

When one is in submission to leadership the spiritual dominion of the leader is imparted into their life. In Exodus, God placed the spirit Moses had in the elders. God's favor flows through leaders into those in submission. God has placed everyone in a position of submission. Romans 13 is not merely about political and civil authority. It applies to spiritual authority in the church and kingdom of God.

> For there is no authority except from God, and the authorities that exist are appointed by God. 2 Therefore whoever resists the authority resists the ordinance of God, and those who resist will bring judgment on themselves. (Romans 13:1-2)

In the Old Testament Joshua led the fight against the Amalekites. Moses, overlooking the battle, held his hands over the field of battle. Aaron and Hur aided Moses by sustaining his hands as the battle progressed. Joshua, fighting and in submission to Moses, was a partaker of his dominion. Spiritual authority was imparted into Joshua. Eventually Joshua led the entire nation into the Promised Land. Elisha labored under the leadership and ministry of Elijah. Elisha received a double portion of the anointing of Elijah.

Being born to rule is only part of the story. Adam and Eve were given dominion. When they violated God's rule, disaster struck. Hebrews notes the importance of authority and submission:

> Remember those who rule over you, who have spoken the word of God to you, whose faith follow, considering the outcome of their conduct ... (17) Obey those who rule over you, and be submissive, for they watch out for your souls, as those who must give account. Let them do so with joy and not with grief, for that would be unprofitable for you. (Hebrews 13:7, 17)

The Gadarene was delivered. His body was set free. He was no longer running naked and cutting himself with stones. He also had to be transformed in his mind to activate dominion in life. Deliverance was not all God had for this man.

> I beseech you therefore, brethren, by the mercies of God, that you present your bodies a living sacrifice, holy, acceptable to God, which is your reasonable service. 2 And do not be conformed to this world, but be transformed by the renewing of your mind, that you may prove what is that good and acceptable and perfect will of God. (Romans 12:1-2)

The Gadarene had to shift his thinking. His desire was to immediately go with Jesus. The issue of his future is what Jesus brought into focus. Deliverance has a purpose. When Jesus was forced to leave the area of Decapolis, he wanted to go with Jesus. Deliverance is more than being free of one's past. It is not for a change of venue or a group of new friends. Deliverance is not just having a support group. Deliverance does not automatically translate into dominion.

Jesus focuses the issue for the Gadarene. You cannot live in dominion if you have no purpose. The Gadarene desires to get in the boat and leave with Jesus and the disciples. Jesus forbids this. Jesus does so because there is a higher purpose for the Gadarene's life. His testimony has value in the regions that know him and who are lost without Christ.

Deliverance becomes dominion when the Gadarene hears Jesus say, "No." He responds in obedience. His life becomes one of purpose in submission to Jesus. It is possible only when we surrender to Jesus. When submission to the will of God is positively responded to, dominion is established. Wherever and whenever we surrender to God's will, we gain dominion. Wherever and whenever we resist God and God's will we lose dominion.

This is the dynamic of dominion. What happens when our plans and goals are not rubber-stamped by God? Is our reaction childish? Do we pout, get mad, throw a fit and say, "Forget it?" Is it possible that God's plan is greater than we could ask or think? Pastor Gooding was asked twice to think about taking over a particular church. Twice he said, "No." A third time he was asked and feeling some pressure, said, "Yes." It didn't work out as well as he had hoped. It did serve God's purposes. It was important personally, because it broadened and established a new dominion in ministry. It has proven fruitful in the years following.

You cannot say, "No," to God without the loss of dominion. And without dominion there is a loss of destiny. It is important to see that destiny is not simply a destination. It is not simply an arrival point. Destiny is about who you have become when you arrive.

We are social learners. We learn values, priorities and heritage from our church culture. The dynamic of church life is not simply the learning of biblical truths and doctrines. Many catechisms are established with the idea that if you believe these things then you are saved. But being forced to believe things you don't understand or really believe is not salvation. Deliverance and dominion are internal issues of the heart and soul. They are revelations of the inner man. Revelation changes your life. It is supernatural. It comes into your soul as reality. It is deeper and more commanding of your life than memorizing facts and figures, names and dates and outcomes.

In obedience to God you find a dominion and you find aspects of God that doesn't come from books. Patrick Johnson and his wife left their successful ministry to pioneer in China. She had a successful career teaching and he was a successful and in demand evangelist with overseas and conference ministry. They chose to leave these and to pioneer a church in China. When he came home on furlough he talked with Campbell and said, "Pastor, I discovered in China a God that I never knew."

Deliverance is not a *carte blanche* ticket to all God has. Deliverance opens the door to opportunity. It comes with freedom, but not freedom only to be free. Is it possible that many who are delivered never see the destiny possible in Jesus? Dominion is not a set of beliefs. It is a revelation of what God can do if we will live in his presence. All things are possible to those who believe. It is not just to those who memorize some biblical promises. It happens when we surrender to God. When our desire becomes a desire to live in Christ, and to have Christ live in us, that's revelation. It is the spiritual dynamic of dominion.

Joseph C. Campbell and John W. Gooding

CHAPTER 9

EPILOGUE

We learn from life. Pastor Campbell, and others have often said, "If you can control your mind you can control your destiny." We process life in our minds. We can process them through the lens of rejection, anger, disappointment, unbelief or a myriad of other issues that have affected us.

James Allen was born in Leicester, England in 1864. He was orphaned, self-educated and earned a living as a clerical worker. An avid reader and student he gave up the clerical position to write in 1902. He wrote 19 inspirational books until an early death in 1912 at 48. His most influential work was *As a Man Thinketh*, in 1902.[1] It was the foundation for most of the motivational books of the 20th century. Tony Robbins, Dale Carnegie, Norman Vincent Peale and others followed James Allen's theme. His title was from Proverbs,

> Do not eat the bread of a miser, Nor desire his delicacies; 7 For as he thinks in his heart, so is he. "Eat and drink!" he says to you, But his heart is not with you. (Proverbs 23:6-7)

Do you see it? There is something wrong with the miser. It is in his heart (or mind)—not just his words. His mind is saying something else. His mind is the determining factor. He is a miser because he is a miser in his head. The Bible brings this truth to light in two important passages. One text is in Philippians:

> Finally, brethren, whatever things are true, whatever things are noble, whatever things are just, whatever things are pure, whatever things are lovely, whatever things are of good report, if there is any virtue

and if there is anything praiseworthy—meditate on these things. 9 The things which you learned and received and heard and saw in me, these do, and the God of peace will be with you. (Philippians 3:8-9)

And then Paul, speaking of the spiritual war in 2nd Corinthians writes:

For the weapons of our warfare are not carnal but mighty in God for pulling down strongholds, 5 casting down arguments and every high thing that exalts itself against the knowledge of God, bringing every thought into captivity to the obedience of Christ,
(2 Corinthians 10:4-5)

What we think and meditate on are important to who we are. Our peace depends on what goes on in our mind. Every thought must be brought to obedience in God. Crises are often the place of your most intense testing. In the Garden of Gethsemane Jesus faced the two greatest tests in life, the struggle for faith and the battle of temptation. You must survive both of these as a believer. Survival depends on submission to God's choices and decisions. Even when the flesh is weak, submission is necessary. Submission begins in the mind.

Campbell said, "God saved me. He did not save my mind. I needed to be transformed." Of course, it did not mean he was only partially saved. There are only two categories of people—the saved and the unsaved. It was true, however, there was a lot of work to be done in the "renewing of his mind." When the mind is surrendered to God the demonic is defeated. This is dominion. When you submit to the will of God then you gain dominion. Whatever area of your mind—fears, hopes, offenses, and rejections—as you surrender to God, they become an area of dominion.

Jesus said he did only what he saw and heard from his father. We all need strong examples. This is largely obtained in the church atmosphere and context. It is also necessary to control our minds by bringing them into captivity and to the obedience of Christ. Paul writes, "Let this mind be in you which was also in Christ Jesus (Philippians 2:5)." In Romans he writes, "Oh, the depth of the riches both of the wisdom and knowledge of God! How unsearchable are His judgments and His ways past finding out! 34 'For who has known the mind of the Lord' (Romans 11:33-34)?" The mind of the Lord is critical in the unknown and perplexing arenas of life.

While ministering in a remote area of the Philippines in March 1983, Pastor Campbell got a call from home. His daughter Gail had died in a hiking accident. His mind went crazy. Fellow pastors arranged for a plane to pick him up and get him to Manila for an international flight home. A friend arranged for him to get three seats in economy for the flight to the US. Going into shock he had simply grabbed his bag and headed for the small plane. He remembers a demonic looking procession coming across the field where he was going to board the small plane. By the time he finally boarded the international flight he said, "My mind was just shredded." Alone in the economy section of the plane, the demonic voices in his head said, "This never happened to you when you were a sinner." Almost mockingly and to torment at the same time, the voices said, "So, this is what the ministry is all about." They spoke doubt about God and the ministry saying, "You are doing God's work here. How could God allow such a thing to happen?" Indeed, more than one ministry has been derailed by similar tragedies and demonic accusations.

When Joe was on his way home across the Pacific, he was trying to process the events and the few details he knew. But his mind was a mess. He was in denial, in prayer, in agony and tormented by hell. But he heard God speak to him, "Son, trust me. I know the end from the beginning." Joe made a decision. He said, "I chose to believe and trust God."

The voices ceased.

When your world is framed by faith it is hard for the demonic to get in your head. It is difficult for the hellish world to get into a life and mind framed in God's word by faith.

In *The Influential Mind*, Tali Sharot—former member of the Israeli Air Force, neuroscientist and author—tells of a social learning experiment using her baby, Livia. She placed a number of objects in plain view around her to see what she would reach for first. Time and again, if the cell-phone was in the mix, little Livia would reach for it. She would promptly put it in her mouth and begin to chew. Shraot's anecdote about Livia opens her discussion of how we learn. Livia wanted the iPhone because from her first days "she had observed her parents constantly interacting with it with great interest."[2] Sharot continues, "It suggests that we are born with an automatic predisposition to learn from those around us. The tendency is instinctive, a reflex—an impulse for social learning."

> The human brain is engineered to acquire knowledge within a social context. We learn almost everything—from what item is most valuable to how to peel an orange—from observing other people's behavior. We imitate, assimilate, and adopt; and we often do this without awareness. The advantage of this setup is that we need not learn only from our own limited experiences with the environment but can also pick up information or techniques from the experience of many others. This means that we can learn quickly, rather than only through the slow process of trial and error. (153)

In other words, we learn by watching other people and how they live. We are influenced and made what we are by our cultures. We are not just about our *DNA*. We almost universally claim to learn our own lessons and we desire to be different. Although, most claim to make up their own minds, we uniformly dress and speak similarly. The desire to be different and the influence of social learning result in many people, if not most, making the same "distinctly different" choices. We drive on the same roads, the same kinds of vehicles to the same places. Despite what we say, those around us have influence. Statistically, we cannot all be less susceptible than the average person to social influence. Much of what influences us operates under the radar. Sharot says we are not all little Mahatma Gandhi's or Albert Einstein's.

We learn from the social contexts of our lives. We learn from our families, friends, peers and co-workers. Chances are very good that if you decided in your youth that you would never be like your father in a crisis at school, in marriage, or on the job that a good deal of how you responded was "father-like." Your family stamps you with its image. Other aspects of culture also seek to stamp you and influence your behavior. Your neighborhood, your friends, your church, and your society all stamp or mark you in some way in life.

We learn in life far more than we do from books. We are social learners. And we learn from the events of life.

This idea of social pressure makes us uncomfortable. It is portrayed as a weakness in the modern world. It was, however, distinctly how Jesus taught. He did not establish a Bible school or seminary. Jesus called the disciples to follow him and become like him. Jesus intentionally influenced them to the right behaviors and beliefs. This is interesting because today we learn from our culture. Jesus made disciples by influencing them away from their cultural learning. His disciples, his "learners," learned to be like him. This "mystery" of influence is at the heart of discipleship and a key to incorporating dominion in one's life. It is why example is so powerful.

Throughout this book it has been repeatedly noted that the mind is crucial. We have been shaped by our culture. Deliverance has broken the chains of bondage. Deliverance sets one free from the sin that so easily captured us. Deliverance gives us opportunity to live a new life in Christ. It is the power of God doing the heavy lifting of salvation. We are asked, then, to walk worthy of Christ and his calling. This is dominion. Dominion requires the mindsets of the world to be cast down and destroyed. It is often the most difficult thing to demolish what we have learned from the cultures we live in. It is not hard physically. It is something that occurs in the mind.

Salvation requires new role models and new behaviors. These are found in the culture of the kingdom of God. This culture, today, is found in the House of God, the church. It is the body of Christ. The mindset of the world sees church as merely an old and out-of-date tradition. The people of God, however, are the manifest body of Christ. The assembly of God's people coming together as the church, is God's chosen means of accomplishing his purposes on earth. It is the place of discipleship. It is the place of intentional influence for a new life. There is no substitute for learning how to live the Christian life than a good, gospel preaching and teaching church. It provides the culture for renewing the mind and transformation.

It is not mind over matter. It is not positive thinking. It is not imaging. The world does not need more bent spoons. It is submission to the word of God. It is about framing your life in faith—no matter what happens. God remains faithful. If you can believe, all things are possible. Man is incurably religious and seeks experiences rather than truth. To process life properly, one must have a definite connection to God's word. This was true of Daniel. By reading the scrolls, he knew God's time for the Babylonian captivity would end. He then set his face to pray. His prayer was framed in faith by the word of God. His prayer was connected to the known will of God. Daniel understood God would keep his promises and deliver from captivity.

Daniel, and all the heroes of faith, had to guard their minds against the vocabulary and attitudes of their cultures. Often they experienced rejection. Often they experienced times of perplexity and uncertain futures. They had to be aware of the word of God and make their prayers accordingly. Controlling their minds was not about self-will or dreaming their way to success. In fact, it wasn't about success at all. It was about obedience to the high calling of God in Christ Jesus. Their prayers were shaped by their experience with God and his word. Christianity is about revelation. It is a revelation from heaven. It is a revelation of Jesus Christ, Lord and savior of the world.

When Joe was born again, it was joyous occasion for him. It was not joyous for his mother and father. Joe was born while is father was in the military during WWII. His father became a bingeing alcoholic. He had long periods of sobriety and would binge drink. Joe had to, at times, lead him to the door of their home. After Joe got home from the Philippines, they held the funeral for Gail. His mother and father attended the services and both were born again. He asked, "Why did you wait to get saved until now?" He had witnessed to them over and over and they always resisted salvation. "Why now?" he asked. It was because they saw how Connie responded during the crisis of Gail's death. They watched Connie's reactions. They saw she understood what a joy it was to have Gail for fifteen years. It moved them to such a degree they received God's salvation.

If you control your mind in faith through the crises you experience, God will move into the arena of your life. You will also impact the lives and destinies of others. Dominion leads to destiny.

> You will keep him in perfect peace,
> Whose mind is stayed on You,
> Because he trusts in You.
> (Isaiah 26:3)

REFERENCES

CHAPTER 1

[1] M. Scott Peck. *The People of the Lie.* (Touchstone: NY). 1983. 182-183

[2] Peck. 195-196.

[3] Maarten J. Paul. "Leviathan (#4293)." *in* Willem A. VanGemeren, ed. *Dictionary of Old Testament Theology and Exegesis.* 1997. Electronic Edition.

[4] Scott Cacciola. *NYTimes.* August 30, 2018. B7.

[5] National Sources of Law Enforcement Employment Data (2016).

[6] Jacquelle Crowe. *This Changes Everything: How the Gospel Transforms the Teen Years.* (Crossway: Wheaton, IL). 2017. 18.

CHAPTER 2

[1] Dallas Willard. *Living in Christ's Presence.* (IVP: Downers Grove, IL). 2014. 26-27.

[2] Charles Kraft. *Christianity With Power.* (Vine Books: Eugene, OR). 1989. 26.

[3] Willard. 46.

[4] Russell Moore. *The Storm-Tossed Family: How the Cross Reshapes the Home.* (B&H: Nashville). 2018.

[5] Cornelius Plantinga. *Not the Way it is Supposed to Be.* (Eerdmans: Grand Rapids, MI). 1995. 56

[6] Plantinga. 52.

CHAPTER 3

[1] Brian Christian and Tom Griffiths. *Algorithms to Live By: The Computer Science of Human Decisions.* (Henry Holt and Company: NY). 2016. 9.

[2] Star Parker. *Uncle Sam's Plantation.* (Nelson: Nashville). 2003. 3.

[3] David McCullough. *The American Spirit: Who We Are and What We Stand For.* (Simon and Schuster: NY). 2017. 59-69.

[4] Parker. 41.

[5] "How to be Happier." *The Week.* August 17, 24, 2018. 36-37. Article excerpted from the *New York Times Magazine,* by Adam Sternbergh.

[6] Hedy Kober, *in* Adam Sternbergh. "Read This Story and Get Happier." *New York Times Magazine, The Cut.* Thecut.com. Accessed May 8, 2019.

[7] Anonymous. *Inspiring Quotes.* #2206.

CHAPTER 4

[1] Michael Lewis. *The Undoing Project.* (W.W. Norton: NY). 2017.

[2] Jim Holt. *New York Times: Sunday Book Review.* "Two Brains Running." November 27, 2011. BR16.

[3] Dan Ariely. *Predictably Irrational: The Hidden Forces that Shape Our Decisions.* (HarperCollins: NY). 2009.

[4] Steven D. Levitt and Stephen J. Dubner. *Freakonomics: A Rogue Economist Explores the Hidden Side of Everything.* (HarperCollins: NY). 2005.

[5] Richard H. Thaler and Cass R. Sunstein. *Nudge: Improving Decisions about Health, Wealth, and Happiness.* (Penguin Books: NY). 2009.

[6] John G. Butler. *Ruth: The Ancestress of Christ.* Bible Biography Series #20. (LBC Publications: Clinton, IA). 1999. 7.

[7] Clayton M. Christensen. *HBR's On Managing Yourself.* 1-12.

CHAPTER 5

[1] David A. Hubbard. *The Communicators Commentary: Proverbs.* (Word Books: Dallas). 1991. 271.

[2] Tali Sharot. *The Influential Mind.* (Henry Holt: NY). 2017. 6-9.

CHAPTER 6

[1] David Wells, *Courage to be Protestant.* (William B. Eerdmans: Grand Rapids, MI). 2008. 161.

[2] Walter Brueggemann. *Money and Possessions.* (Westminster John Knox Press: Louisville). 2016. xix-xxi.

CHAPTER 7

[1] Brian Christian and Tom Griffiths. *Algorithms to Live By: The Computer Science of Human Decisions.* (Henry Holt and Company: NY). 2016.

[2] Bobdylan.com/gotta-serve-somebody. Accessed 4/7/2019.

[3] Watchman Nee. *The Latent Power of the Soul.* (Christian Fellowship Publishers). Audio-book. 2014.

[4] David W. Baker. *The NIV Application Commentary: Joel, Obadiah, Malachi.* (Zondervan: Grand Rapids, MI). 2006. 46.

[5] Charles Spurgeon. *Treasury of David.* (Henrickson: Peabody, MA). II:192.

CHAPTER 8

[1] Businessinsider.com. 2016-1. John Sculley. Accessed 5/1/2019.

[2] Bethany Mandel. *NYPost*. 06/02/2018. Jessica Lahey. *The Gift of Failure*. (Harper: NY). 2016.

[3] Barbara Crossette. *NYTimes*. October 30, 1987. A8.

CHAPTER 9

[1] James Allen. *As a Man Thinketh*. (Jon Rose: Langhorn, PA). 1902.

[2] Tali Sharot. Chapter 7, 149-171.

Made in the USA
Columbia, SC
01 July 2019